Guitar Chord Songbook

Christmas Carols

ISBN 978-0-634-05057-2

HAL•LEONARD®
CORPORATION

7777 W. BLUEMOUND RD. P.O. BOX 13819 MILWAUKEE, WI 53213

Visit Hal Leonard Online at
www.halleonard.com

Contents

All My Heart This Night Rejoices

Words and Music by Johann Ebeling
and Catherine Winkworth

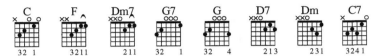

Verse 1

    C   **F**   **C**
All my heart this night rejoices,

    Dm7 G7   **C**
As I hear, far and near,

    G   **D7 G**
Sweetest angel voices.

    Dm   **Dm7**   **G7**   **C**
"Christ is born," their choirs are singing,

       G   **C**
Till the air ev'rywhere

   C7   **Dm7 G7** **C**
Now with joy is ringing.

	C		F	C

Verse 2   Hark, a voice from yonder manger,

Dm7 G7 C
Soft and sweet, doth entreat,

G   D7 G
"Flee from woe and danger.

Dm   Dm7   G7 C
Brethren, come from all grieves you.

G7   C
You are freed; all you need

C7   Dm7 G7 C
I will surely give you."

C   F   C
Verse 3   Come then, let us hasten yonder.

Dm7 G   C
Here let all,__ great and small,

G   D7 G
Kneel in awe and wonder.

Dm   Dm7   G7   C
Love Him who with love is yearning.

G   C
Hail the star that from far

C7   Dm7   G7 C
Bright with hope is burning.

Angels from the Realms of Glory

Words by James Montgomery
Music by Henry T. Smart

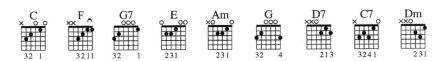

Verse 1

    C
Angels from the realms of glory,

F   **C**   **G7**   **C**
Wing your flight o'er all the earth;

                E
Ye who sang creation's story,

Am   **G** **D7** **G**
Now proclaim Mes - si - ah's birth.

Chorus 1

G7
Come and worship!

C7   **F**
Come and worship!

Dm   **G7**   **C**
Worship Christ the newborn King!

GUITAR CHORD SONGBOOK

Verse 2

C
Shepherds in the fields abiding,

F   C   G7   C
Watching o'er your flocks by night,

                    E
God with man is now residing;

Am   G D7 G
Yonder shines the in - fant Light.

Chorus 2   Repeat Chorus 1

Verse 3

C
Sages, leave your contemplations,

F   C   G7   C
Brighter visions beam a - far,

                    E
Seek the great Desire of nations,

Am   G D7 G
Ye have seen His natal star.

Chorus 3   Repeat Chorus 1

Verse 4

C
Saints before the altar bending,

F   C   G7   C
Watching long in hope and fear,

                  E
Suddenly the Lord, descending,

Am   G   D7 G
In His temple shall ap - pear.

Chorus 4   Repeat Chorus 1

Angels We Have Heard on High

Traditional French Carol
Translated by James Chadwick

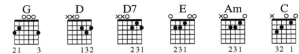

Verse 1

G   D G
Angels we have heard on high,

      D7 G
Singing sweetly o'er the plains,

       D G
And the mountains in reply

     D7 G
Echoing their joyous strains.

Chorus 1

G E Am D G C D7
Glo - - - - - - ria.

G   D
In excelsis Deo,

G E Am D G C D7
Glo - - - - - - ria.

G   D7 G
In excelsis De - o.

Verse 2

G   D   G
Shepherds, why this jubilee?

           D7   G
Why your joyous strains prolong?

           D   G
What the gladsome tidings be

           D7   G
Which inspire your heavenly song?

Chorus 2   Repeat Chorus 1

Verse 3

G   D   G
Come to Bethlehem and see

           D7   G
Him whose birth the angels sing.

          D   G
Come adore on bended knee

           D7   G
Christ the Lord, the newborn King.

Chorus 3   Repeat Chorus 1

Verse 4

G   D   G
See within a manger laid

           D7   G
Jesus, Lord of heav'n and earth!

          D   G
Mary, Joseph, lend your aid;

           D7   G
With us sing our Savior's birth.

Chorus 4   Repeat Chorus 1

As With Gladness Men of Old

Words by William Chatterton Dix
Music by Conrad Kocher

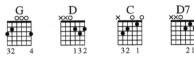

Verse 1

G   D G C   D7 G
As with gladness men of old

C   G C D   G
Did the guiding star behold;

      D G   C   D7 G
As with joy they hailed its light,

C   G C   D   G
Leading onward, beaming bright;

           D   G
So, most gracious Lord, may we

C G   C G D G
Evermore be led to Thee.

Verse 2

G   D G C   D7 G
As with joyful steps they sped

C   G C D   G
To that lowly manger bed,

      D   G   C   D7 G
There to bend the knee before

C   G   C D   G
Him whom heav'n and earth adore;

          D   G
So may we with willing feet

C G   C G D G
Ever seek thy mercy seat.

Verse 3

```
G     D   G    C   D7  G
```
As they of - fered gifts most rare

```
C    G   C   D      G
```
At that manger rude and bare;

```
      D  G   C D7 G
```
So may we with holy joy,

```
C       G   C   D     G
```
Pure and free from sin's alloy,

```
           D       G
```
All our costliest treasures bring,

```
C      G   C  G  D  G
```
Christ, to Thee, our heav'nly King.

Verse 4

```
G   D G   C D7 G
```
Holy Jesus, ev'ry day

```
C    G C D      G
```
Keep us in the narrow way;

```
      D  G  C     D7 G
```
And when earthly things are past,

```
C       G C    D      G
```
Bring our ransomed souls at last

```
              D     G
```
Where they need no star to guide,

```
C      G   C  G D G
```
Where no clouds Thy glory hide.

Away in a Manger

Traditional
Words by John T. McFarland (v.3)
Music by James R. Murray

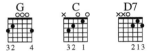

Verse 1

      G   C   G
Away in a manger, no crib for His bed,

      D7   G
The little Lord Jesus lay down His sweet head;

                        C   G
The stars in the bright sky looked down where He lay,

      D7   G   C   D7 G
The little Lord Jesus, asleep in the hay.

Verse 2

```
         G                    C     G
The cattle are lowing, the baby awakes,
         D7                 G
But little Lord Jesus no crying He makes.
                           C            G
I love Thee, Lord Jesus! Look down from the sky,
         D7      G      C      D7 G
And stay by my side until morning is nigh.
```

Verse 3

```
         G                    C     G
Be near me, Lord Jesus; I ask Thee to stay
         D7                 G
Close by me forever, and love me, I pray.
                           C      G
Bless all the dear children in Thy tender care,
         D7      G      C      D7  G
And take us to heaven, to live with Thee there.
```

Break Forth, O Beauteous, Heavenly Light

Words by Johann Rist
Translated by John Troutbeck
Melody by Johann Schop
Arranged by J.S. Bach

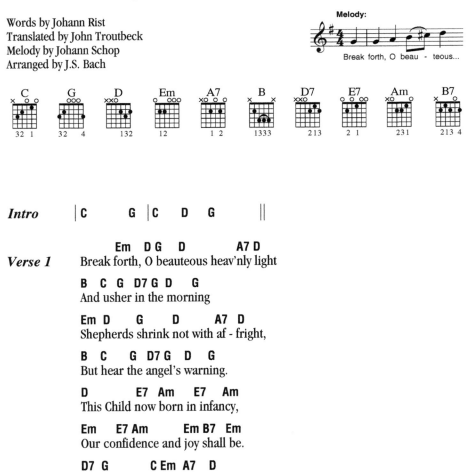

Intro | C   G | C   D   G ||

Verse 1

        Em D G D   A7 D
Break forth, O beauteous heav'nly light

B C G D7 G D   G
And usher in the morning

Em D   G   D   A7 D
Shepherds shrink not with af - fright,

B C   G D7 G D   G
But hear the angel's warning.

D   E7 Am   E7   Am
This Child now born in infancy,

Em   E7 Am   Em B7 Em
Our confidence and joy shall be.

D7 G   C Em A7   D
The power of Satan breaking;

G   C   D7 C G D G
Our peace eternal making.

GUITAR CHORD SONGBOOK

Verse 2

      Em   D G D   A7 D   B
He comes to reconcile all men and

C   G D7 G D G   Em   D G
Men to God forever He comes to mend.

D   A7 D B C G D7 G   D G
The cords of love wherever sin does sever.

D   E7 Am   E7   Am
He is the light upon our way;

Em   E7 Am Em B7 Em
To bring us to the promised day.

D7 G   C Em A7 D
This Child God's incarnation;

G   C   D7 C G D G
Our hope and our salvation!

Bring a Torch, Jeannette, Isabella

17th Century French Provençal Carol

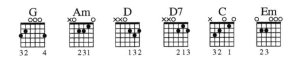

Verse 1

     G   Am   D
Bring a torch, Jeannette, Isa - bella,

     G   D7   G
Bring a torch, come swiftly and run.

                             D
Christ is born, tell the folk of the village,

     C   G   D7   G D
Jesus is sleeping in His cradle,

     Em D G   D   G
Ah, ah, beautiful is the Mother,

     Em D G   D   G
Ah, ah, beautiful is her Son.

Verse 2

     G   Am   D
Hasten now, good folk of the village,

     G   D7   G
Hasten now, the Christ Child to see.

                            D
You will find Him asleep in a manger,

     C   G   D7   G D
Quietly come and whisper softly,

     Em   D   G   D   G
Hush, hush, peacefully now He slumbers,

     Em   D   G   D   G
Hush, hush, peacefully now He sleeps.

Christ Was Born on Christmas Day

Traditional

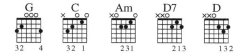

Verse

G   C G
Christ was born on Christmas Day,

       C G
Wreath the holly, twine the bay;

Am D7 G D
Christus natus hodie;

    G   C G D7 G
The Babe, the Son, the Holy One of Mary.

A Child Is Born in Bethlehem

14th-Century Latin Text adapted by Nicolai F.S. Grundtvig
Traditional Danish Melody

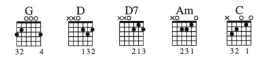

Verse 1	**G** A Child is born in Bethlehem,
	D G D7 G In Beth - le - hem;
	Am G D Am G C And joy is in Je - ru - sa - lem,
	D G Am G D7 G Alleluja, Al - le - lu - ja!

Verse 2	**G** A lowly maiden all alone,
	D G D7 G So all a - lone,
	Am G D Am G C Gave birth to God's own Ho - ly Son.
	D G Am G D7 G Alleluja, Al - le - lu - ja!

Verse 3

G
She chose a manger for His bed,

D   G D7 G
For Jesus' bed.

Am   G   D Am G   C
God's angels sang for joy o'erhead,

D G   Am G D7 G
Alleluja, Al - le - lu - ja!

Verse 4

G
Give thanks and praise eternally,

D G   D7   G
E - ter - nal - ly,

Am G   D Am G C
To God, the Holy Trin - i - ty.

D G   Am G D7 G
Alleluja, Al - le - lu - ja!

Child Jesus

Words by Hans Christian Andersen
Music by Niels Gade

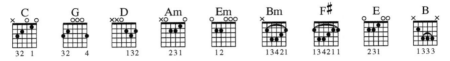

C	G	D	Am	Em	Bm	F#	E	B
32 1	32 4	132	231	12	13421	134211	231	1333

Verse 1

     C G   C G D
Child Jesus in a manger lay,

G   C Am G D G
Yet Heaven was His own.____

     C G   C G D
His lowly pillow was of straw,

G D   Em Bm F#   Bm
And 'round Him no light shone._____

D G   D E Am D G
But Heaven sent a star so bright,

       C   B   Em
And oxen kissed His feet that night,

C D Em F# Bm
Alleluja, Alleluja,

Em C D G
Al - le - lu - ja!

Verse 2

    C G   **C G D**
O crippled soul be glad today,

G   **C**   **Am G D** **G**
Cast out your bit - ter pain.____

    C G   **C G**   **D**
For Bethle'm's Babe will show the way,

G D **Em Bm** **F#**   **Bm**
We heav'nly bliss can gain._____

D G   **D**   **E** **Am D G**
Let us with child-like heart and mind,

        C   **B**   **Em**
Seek now the Son of God to find.

C D **Em F#** **Bm**
Alleluja, Alleluja,

Em C **D** **G**
Al - le - lu - ja!

Come, All Ye Shepherds

Traditional Czech Text
Traditional Moravian Melody

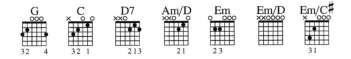

Verse

G   C G   C G   D7 G
Come, all ye shepherds such wonders en - thrall.

          Am/D G   Am/D G   D7 G
Come where the__ young Child is_____ laid in a stall.

Em   Em/D Em/C#   D7
This day to us__ a Savior is given,

Em   Em/D   Em/C#   D7
Whom, God on high hath sent down from heaven.

G   D7 G
Hal - le - lu - jah!

The First Noël

17th Century English Carol
Music from W. Sandys' Christmas Carols

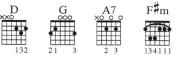

Verse 1
      D   **G**   **D**
The first Noël, the angel did say,

        G   **D**   **A7**   **D**
Was to certain poor shepherds in fields as they lay;

            G   **D**
In fields where they lay keeping their sheep,

     G   **D**   **A7**   **D**
On a cold winter's night that was so deep.

Chorus 1
     D   **F#m**   **G**   **D**
Noël, No - ël,___ No - ël,___ No - ël,

G   **A7**   **D** **A7** **D**
Born is the King of Is - ra - el.

Verse 2
      D   **G**   **D**
They looked up and saw a star

        G   **D**   **A7**   **D**
Shining in the East, beyond them far;

           G   **D**
And to the earth it gave great light,

     G   **D**   **A7**   **D**
And so it continued both day and night.

Chorus 2   Repeat Chorus 1

Verse 3

      D   **G**   **D**
And by the light of that same star,

      G   **D**   **A7**   **D**
Three wise men came from country far;

         G   **D**
To seek for a King was their intent,

      G   **D**   **A7**   **D**
And to follow the star wherever it went.

Chorus 3   Repeat Chorus 1

Verse 4

      D   **G**   **D**
This star drew nigh to the northwest,

      G   **D**   **A7**   **D**
O'er Bethlehem it took its rest;

         G   **D**
And there it did both stop and stay,

      G   **D**   **A7**   **D**
Right over the place where Jesus lay.

Chorus 4   Repeat Chorus 1

Verse 5

        D   G   D
Then entered in those wise men three,

      G   D   A7   D
Full reverently upon their knee;

                G   D
And offered there in His presence,

      G   D   A7   D
Their gold, and myrrh, and frankincense.

Chorus 5   Repeat Chorus 1

Verse 6

        D   G   D
Then let us all with one accord

      G   D   A7   D
Sing praises to our heav'nly Lord,

                  G   D
That hath made heav'n and earth of naught,

      G   D   A7   D
And with His blood mankind hath brought.

Chorus 6   Repeat Chorus 1

Come, Thou Long Expected Jesus

Words by Charles Wesley
Music adapted by Henry J. Gauntlett

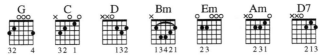

Verse 1

G   C   D
Come Thou long-expected Jesus,

G   D   G
Born to set Thy people free.

                C   D
From our fears and sins release us,

G   D   G
Let us find our rest in Thee.

Bm   Em   Am D7
Israel's strength and consolation,

G   Em Am   D
Hope of all the earth Thou art.

G   D7 G D7
Dear desire of ev'ry nation,

G   C   D7   G
Joy of ev'ry longing heart.

Verse 2	G C D

G   C   D
Born Thy people to deliver,

G   D   G
Born a child and yet a king.

**   C   D**
Born to reign in us forever,

G   D   G
Now Thy gracious kingdom bring.

Bm   Em   Am   D7
By Thine own eternal Spirit,

G   Em   Am   D
Rule in all our hearts alone.

G   D7   G   D7
By Thine all sufficient merit,

G   C   D7   G
Raise us to Thy glorious throne.

Coventry Carol

Words by Robert Croo
Traditional English Melody

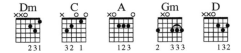

Verse 1

      Dm   C   A
Lullay, thou little tiny Child,

Dm   Gm Dm
By by, lully lullay.

      C   Gm A
Lullay, thou little tiny Child,

Dm   Gm D
By by, lully lullay.

GUITAR CHORD SONGBOOK

Verse 2

```
    Dm              C     A
    O sisters too, how may we do,

    Dm      Gm        Dm
    For to preserve this day.

          C                Gm      A
    This poor youngling for whom we sing,

    Dm     Gm  D
    By by, lully lullay.
```

Verse 3

```
    Dm              C     A
    Herod the king, in his raging,

    Dm      Gm        Dm
    Charged he hath this day.

          C            Gm      A
    His men of might, in his own sight,

    Dm          Gm    D
    All young children to slay.
```

Verse 4

```
    Dm                C      A
    That woe is me, poor Child for Thee!

    Dm      Gm        Dm
    And ever morn and day,

          C           Gm      A
    For thy parting nor say nor sing,

    Dm     Gm  D
    By by, lully lullay.
```

Deck the Hall

Traditional Welsh Carol

Melody:
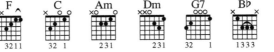

Deck   the   hall   with...

F   C   Am   Dm   G7   B♭
xx   x o o   x o   o   x x o   o o o   x
3 2 1 1 3 2 1   2 3 1   2 3 1   3 2   1 1 3 3 3

Verse 1

F
Deck the hall with boughs of holly,

C   F   C   F
Fa la la la la, la la la la.

'Tis the season to be jolly,

C   F   C   F
Fa la la la la, la la la la.

C   F
Don we now our gay apparel,

Am   Dm   G7   C
Fa la la, la la la, la la la.

F
Troll the ancient Yuletide carol,

B♭   F   C   F
Fa la la la la, la la la la.

Verse 2

     F
See the blazing yule before us,

C   F   C   F
Fa la la la la, la la la la.

Strike the harp and join the chorus,

C   F   C   F
Fa la la la la, la la la la.

C   F
Follow me in merry measure,

Am   Dm   G7 C
Fa la la, la la la, la la la.

F
While I tell of Yuletide treasure,

B♭   F   C   F
Fa la la la la, la la la la.

Verse 3

     F
Fast away the old year passes,

C   F   C   F
Fa la la la la, la la la la.

Hail the new, ye lads and lasses,

C   F   C   F
Fa la la la la, la la la la.

C   F
Sing we joyous, all together,

Am   Dm   G7 C
Fa la la, la la la, la la la.

F
Heedless of the wind and weather,

B♭   F   C   F
Fa la la la la, la la la la.

Ding Dong! Merrily on High

French Carol

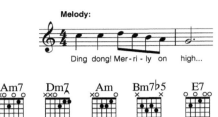

Melody:

Ding dong! Mer - ri - ly on   high...

C   D7   G7   F   Em   Am7   Dm7   Am   Bm7♭5   E7

32 1   213   32 1   3211   23   2 1   211   231   1324   2 1

Verse 1

    C   D7   G7
Ding dong! Merrily on high,

        F   C
In heav'n the bells are ringing.

            D7   G7
Ding dong! Verily the sky

        F   C
Is riv'n with angel singing.

Chorus 1

    Em   Am7   Dm7   G7
Glo -   -   -   -

    Em   Am   Bm7♭5 E7
  -    -   -   -

    Am   Dm7 G7
  -    -   -   - ria,

     F   G7 C
Hosanna in ex - celsis!

GUITAR CHORD SONGBOOK

Verse 2
      C   **D7**   **G7**
      E'en so here below, be - low,

          F   **C**
      Let steeple bells be swungen,

          D7   **G7**
      And io, io, io,

          F   **C**
      By priest and people sungen.

Chorus 2   Repeat Chorus 1

The Friendly Beasts

Traditional English Carol

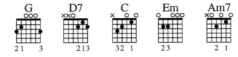

Verse 1

G   D7 G   D7   G
Jesus our brother, kind and good,

         C   D7 G
Was humbly born in a stable rude,

         C   G D7   G
And the friendly beasts a - round Him stood,

     C   G Em   Am7 D7 G
Jesus our brother,__ kind and good.

Verse 2

G   D7 G   D7   G
"I," said the donkey, shaggy and brown,

         C   D7   G
"I carried His mother up hill and down;

         C   G D7   G
I carried her safely to Bethlehem town."

       C G Em Am7 D7 G
"I," said the donkey, shaggy and brown.

Verse 3

```
         G       D7 G      D7       G
      "I," said the cow all white and red,
                  C          D7    G
      "I gave Him my manger for His bed;
                  C  G D7        G
      I gave Him my hay to pillow His head."
                  C   G  Em Am7 D7 G
      "I," said the cow all white and red.
```

Verse 4

```
         G       D7 G       D7   G
      "I," said the sheep with curly horn,
                  C            D7      G
      "I gave Him my wool for His blanket warm;
                  C   G D7        G
      He wore my coat on Christmas morn."
                  C   G   Em  Am7 D7 G
      "I," said the sheep with cur - ly horn.
```

Verse 5

```
         G       D7 G          D7     G
      "I," said the dove from the rafters high,
                  C          D7       G
      "I cooed Him to sleep so He would not cry;
                  C   G D7        G
      We cooed Him to sleep, my mate and I."
                  C   G      Em Am7 D7  G
      "I," said the dove from the raf - ters high.
```

Verse 6

```
       G       D7 G      D7       G
      Thus every beast by some good spell,
                  C      D7   G
      In the stable dark was glad to tell
                  C   G  D7      G
      Of the gift he gave Em - man - u - el,
                  C G   Em  Am7 D7 G
      The gift he gave Em - man - u - el.
```

From the Eastern Mountains

Traditional

Melody:

From the east - ern moun - tains,...

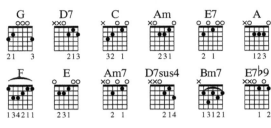

Verse 1

| G | D7 | G | D7 |

From the eastern mountains,

| G | C | D7 |

Pressing on they come,

| Am | E7 | Am | A |

Wise men in their wis - dom,

| G | D7 | G |

To His humble home.

| | F | E | E7 |

Stirred by deep de - vo - tion,

| Am | Am7 | D7sus4 | D7 |

Hasting from a - far,_____

| Am | D7 | Bm7 | E7♭9 |

Ever journ'ing on - ward,

| Am7 | D7 | G |

Guided by a star.

Verse 2

```
G          D7      G  D7
There their Lord and Savior

G        C    D7
Meek and lowly lay,

Am       E7      Am  A
Wondrous light that led them

G       D7      G
Onward on their way.

        F    E   E7
Ever now to lighten

Am      Am7    D7sus4  D7
Nations from a - far,_____

Am      D7     Bm7   E7♭9
As they journey homeward

Am7    D7     G
By that guiding star.
```

Verse 3

```
G         D7  G  D7
Thou who in a manger

G        C    D7
Once hast lowly lain,

Am       E7     Am  A
Who dost now in glo - ry

G       D7      G
O'er all kingdoms reign,

        F    E   E7
Gather in the heathen

Am      Am7    D7sus4  D7
Who in lands a - far_____

Am         D7     Bm7   E7♭9
Ne'er have seen the brightness

Am7    D7     G
Of Thy guiding star.
```

Verse 4

```
G     D7    G   D7
Gather in the outcasts,

G       C      D7
All who have a - stray,

Am        E7       Am  A
Throw Thy radiance o'er them,

G           D7      G
Guide them on their way.

               F     E    E7
Those who never knew Thee,

Am              Am7       D7sus4  D7
Those who have wandered far,_____

Am          D7   Bm7   E7♭9
Guide them by the brightness

Am7  D7      G
Of Thy guiding star.
```

Verse 5

```
G      D7        G   D7
Onward through the darkness

G     C     D7
Of the lonely night,

Am    E7      Am  A
Shining still be - fore them

G        D7   G
With Thy kindly light.

               F      E   E7
Guide them, Jew and Gentile,

Am        Am7     D7sus4  D7
Homeward from a - far,_____

Am          D7   Bm7   E7♭9
Young and old to - geth - er,

Am7  D7      G
By Thy guiding star.
```

Good King Wenceslas

Words by John M. Neale
Music from Piae Cantiones

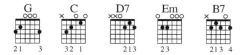

Verse 1

G
Good King Wenceslas looked out

C   D7   G
On the feast of Stephen,

When the snow lay round about,

C   D7   G
Deep and crisp and even;

    D7   G   Em
Brightly shone the moon that night,

C   D7   G
Though the frost was cruel,

    B7   Em   D7
When a poor man came in sight,

G   D7   G   C   G
Gath'ring winter fu - el.

Verse 2

G
"Hither, page, and stand by me,

C   D7   G
If thou know'st it, telling,

Yonder peasant, who is he?

C   D7   G
Where and what his dwelling?"

        D7   G   Em
"Sire, he lives a good league hence,

C   D7   G
Underneath the mountain;

        B7   Em   D7
Right a - gainst the forest fence,

G   D7   G   C G
By Saint Agnes' foun - tain."

Verse 3

G
"Bring me flesh and bring me wine,

C   D7   G
Bring me pine logs hither;

Thou and I will see him dine,

C   D7   G
When we bear them thither."

        D7   G   Em
Page and monarch, forth they went,

C   D7   G
Forth they went to - gether;

        B7   Em   D7
Through the rude wind's wild la - ment

G   D7   G C G
And the bitter weath - er.

Verse 4

G
"Sire, the night is darker now,

C   D7   G
And the wind blows stronger;

Fails my heart, I know not how,

C   D7   G
I can go no longer."

       D7   G   Em
"Mark my footsteps, my good page,

C   D7   G
Tread thou in them boldly;

       B7   Em   D7
Thou shalt find the winter's rage

G   D7   G C G
Freeze thy blood less cold - ly."

Verse 5

G
In his master's steps he trod,

C   D7   G
Where the snow lay dinted;

Heat was in the very sod

C   D7   G
Which the saint had printed.

       D7   G   Em
Therefore, Christian men, be sure,

C   D7   G
Wealth or rank pos - sessing,

       B7   Em   D7
Ye who now will bless the poor,

G   D7   G C G
Shall your - selves find bles - sing.

Fum, Fum, Fum

Traditional Catalonian Carol

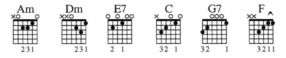

On this joy-ful Christ-mas day...

Am   Dm   E7   C   G7   F

Verse 1

      Am   Dm   E7
On this joyful Christmas day

           Am E7 Am
Sing fum, fum, fum.

               Dm   E7
On this joyful Christmas Day

           Am E7 Am
Sing fum, fum, fum.

          C   G7   C
For a blessed Babe was born

               G7   C
Upon this day at break of morn.

        F   Dm   E7
In a manger poor and lowly

           Am   Dm   E7
Lay the Son of God most holy.

Am E7 Am
Fum, fum, fum.

GUITAR CHORD SONGBOOK

Verse 2

    Am   **Dm E7**
Thanks to God for holidays,

    Am E7 Am
Sing fum, fum, fum.

             Dm E7
Thanks to God for holidays,

    Am E7 Am
Sing fum, fum, fum.

      C   **G7**   **C**
Now we all our voices raise

           G7   **C**
And sing a song of grateful praise,

    F   **Dm**   **E7**
Celebrate in song and story

    Am   **Dm**   **E7**
All the wonders of His glory,

Am E7 Am
Fum, fum, fum.

Gather Around the Christmas Tree

By John H. Hopkins

Gath-er a-round the Christ-mas tree!...

G   D7   B7   Em   Am   D   A7   C

Verse 1

    G   D7   G
Gather around the Christmas tree!

             D7   G
Gather around the Christmas tree!

    B7 Em   Am   D7
Ev - er green have its branches been,

     G   D A7   D
It is king of all the woodland scene.

     D   B7   Em
For Christ, our king is born to - day,

    C   A7   D
His reign shall never pass a - way.

Chorus 1

    G   C   D G   C   D
Ho - san - na, Ho - san - na,

    G D7 Em Am G D7 G
Ho - san - na__ in__ the highest!

Verse 2

G   D7   G
Gather around the Christmas tree!

                D7   G
Gather around the Christmas tree!

     B7 Em   Am   D7
Once the pride of the mountainside,

        G   D A7   D
Now cut down to grace our Christmastide.

G   D   B7   Em
For Christ from heav'n to earth came down

    C   A7   D
To gain, through death, a nobler crown.

Chorus 2   Repeat Chorus 1

Verse 3

G   D7   G
Gather around the Christmas tree!

                D7   G
Gather around the Christmas tree!

     B7 Em   Am   D7
Ev'ry bough has a burden now,

        G   D A7   D
They are gifts of love for us, we trow.

G   D   B7   Em
For Christ is born, his love to show

    C   A7   D
And give good gifts to men below.

Chorus 3   Repeat Chorus 1

Glad Christmas Bells

Traditional American Carol

Am7   D7   C7   B7   Em   G

Verse 1

     Am7   **D7** **C7** **B7** **Em**
Glad Christmas bells, your music tells

     Am7   **D7**   **G**
The sweet and pleasant sto - ry,

      Am7   **D7** **C7 B7**   **Em**
How came to earth, in lowly birth,

     Am7   **D7**   **G**
The Lord of life and glo - ry.

Verse 2

     Am7 D7 **C7 B7**   **Em**
No palace hall, its ceiling tall;

    Am7 **D7**   **G**
is kingly head spread o - ver,

    Am7 D7 **C7 B7**   **Em**
There only stood a_ table rude;

    Am7   **D7**   **G**
The heav'nly Babe to cov - er.

Verse 3

    Am7   **D7 C7 B7**   **Em**
Nor raiment gay as there He lay,

    Am7   **D7**   **G**
Adorn'd the infant stranger;

    Am7   **D7 C7 B7**   **Em**
Poor humble child of mother mild

    Am7   **D7**   **G**
She laid Him in a manger.

Verse 4

    Am7   **D7 C7 B7**   **Em**
But from a - far, a_ splendid star;

    Am7   **D7**   **G**
The wise men westward turning;

    Am7   **D7**   **C7**   **B7**   **Em**
The livelong night saw pure and bright,

    Am7   **D7**   **G**
A - bove His birthplace burning.

Go, Tell It on the Mountain

African-American Spiritual
Verses by John W. Work, Jr.

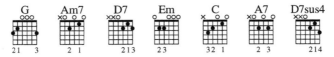

| G | Am7 | D7 | Em | C | A7 | D7sus4 |

Chorus 1

    G
Go tell it on the mountain,

Am7   D7   G   D7
Over the hills and ev'rywhere;

G   Em
Go tell it on the mountain

    Am7 D7   G
That Jesus Christ is born.

Verse 1

      G
While shepherds kept their watching

      C   G
O'er silent flocks by night,

Behold, throughout the heavens,

      Em   A7   D7sus4 D7
There shone a holy light._____

GUITAR CHORD SONGBOOK

Chorus 2   Repeat Chorus 1

                     G
Verse 2   The shepherds feared and trembled

                     C   G
          When, lo! above the earth

          Rang out the angel chorus

               Em   A7   D7sus4 D7
          That hailed our Savior's birth._____

Chorus 3   Repeat Chorus 1

                     G
Verse 3   Down in a lowly manger

                     C   G
          The humble Christ was born,

          And God sent us salvation

               Em   A7   D7sus4 D7
          That blessed Christmas morn._____

Chorus 4   Repeat Chorus 1

God Rest Ye Merry, Gentlemen

19th Century English Carol

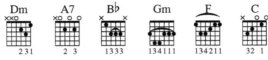

Verse 1

    Dm
God rest ye merry, gentlemen,

          A7
Let nothing you dismay,

    Dm
For Jesus Christ our Savior

    B♭   **A7**
Was born on upon this day,

    Gm   **F**
To save us all from Satan's power

     Dm   **C**
When we were gone a - stray.

Chorus 1

    F   **A7**   **Dm**
O tidings of comfort and joy,

      C
Comfort and joy;

    F   **A7**   **Dm**
O tidings of comfort and joy.

Verse 2

   Dm
In Bethlehem, in Jewry,

       A7
This blessed Babe was born,

   Dm
And laid within a manger

   B♭   **A7**
Up - on this blessed morn;

   Gm   **F**
To which His mother Mary

   Dm   **C**
Did nothing take in scorn.

Chorus 2 Repeat Chorus 1

Verse 3

   Dm
From God our Heav'nly Father,

     A7
A blessed Angel came;

   Dm
And unto certain shepherds

   B♭   **A7**
Brought tidings of the same;

   Gm   **F**
How that in Bethlehem was born

   Dm   **C**
The Son of God by Name.

Chorus 3 Repeat Chorus 1

Going to Bethlehem

Traditional Chilean Carol

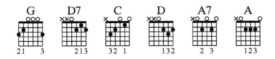

G	D7	C	D	A7	A
21 3	2 1 3	32 1	1 3 2	2 3	1 2 3

                G   **D7**

Verse 1   Good evening, dear, gentle Mary,

                    G

My heart is filled with devotion,

                    D7

My heart is filled with devotion.

                   G

For you and Jesus so lovely,

                 C

A fervent prayer I am off'ring,

  D   **A7**   **D**

A fervent prayer I am off'ring.

                G   **D7**

Chorus 1   Going, going to Bethlehem town,

                    G

Going, going the Baby to see.

                 C

To greet His father, Joseph,

  D   **A7**   **D**

And Mary, on bended knee.

Verse 2
```
               G           D7
        Goodbye to you little Manuel,

                      G
        Until the New Year beginning,

                      D7
        Until the New Year beginning.

                      G
        I'll see you after the shearing,

                               C
        So rich from wool you'll be selling,

         D        A7          D
        So rich from wool you'll be selling.
```

Chorus 2   Repeat Chorus 1

Verse 3
```
         G           D7
        O Mary, Holiest Mother,

                      G
        As pure as flowers unfolding,

                      D7
        As pure as flowers unfolding.

                      G
        I come on this eve of Christmas,

                      C
        Thy love and glory beholding,

         D        A7     D
        Thy love and glory beholding.
```

Chorus 3
```
               G               D7
        Going, going to Bethlehem town,

                          G
        Going, going the Baby to see.

                      C
        To greet His father, Joseph,

         A     D7      G
        And Mary, on bended knee.
```

Good Christian Men, Rejoice

14th Century Latin Text
Translated by John Mason Neale
14th Century German Melody

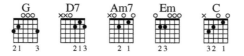

Verse 1

        G
Good Christian men, rejoice,

With heart and soul and voice;

D7   **G**
Give ye heed to what we say:

        Am7 **D7**
News! News! Jesus Christ is born today!

        Em
Ox and ass before Him bow,

    Am7 **D7**   **Em**
And He is in the manger now;

C   **D7**   **G**   **D7**
Christ is born to - day!_____

G   **D7**   **G**
Christ is born to - day!

Verse 2

G
Good Christian men, rejoice,

With heart and soul and voice;

D7   G
Now ye hear of endless bliss;

      Am7 D7
Joy! Joy! Jesus Christ was born for this!

           Em
He has ope'd the heav'nly door,

    Am7 D7   Em
And man is blessed evermore.

C   D7   G   D7
Christ was born for this!_____

G   D7   G
Christ was born for this!

Verse 3

G
Good Christian men, rejoice,

With heart and soul and voice;

D7   G
Now ye need not fear the grave;

      Am7 D7
Peace! Peace! Jesus Christ was born to save!

          Em
Calls you and and calls you all,

   Am7   D7 Em
To gain His everlasting hall.

C   D7   G   D7
Christ was born to save!_____

G   D7   G
Christ was born to save!

Hark! The Herald Angels Sing

Words by Charles Wesley
Altered by George Whitefield
Music by Felix Mendelssohn-Bartholdy
Arranged by William H. Cummings

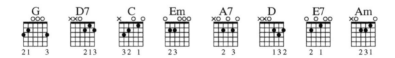

Verse 1

G   D7
Hark! the herald angels sing,

G   C   D7   G
"Glory to the newborn King!

                  Em   A7
Peace on earth, and mercy mild,

D   A7   D
God and sinners reconciled!"

G   C   D7
Joyful, all ye nations, rise,

G   C   D7
Join the triumph of the skies;

C   E7   Am
With th'angelic host proclaim,

D7   G   D7   G
"Christ is born in Bethlehem!"

C   E7   Am
Hark! the herald angels sing,

D7   G   D7   G
"Glory to the newborn King!"

Verse 2

    G   D7
Christ, by highest heav'n a - dored,

G   C D7   G
Christ the everlasting Lord;

                   Em   A7
Late in time be - hold Him come,

D   A7   D
Offspring of the virgin womb.

G   C   D7
Veiled in flesh, the Godhead see:

G   C   D7
Hail, th'incarnate Dei - ty;

C   E7   Am
Pleased, as man, with men to dwell,

D7 G   D7   G
Jesus, our Em-man-u -el!

C   E7   Am
Hark! the herald angels sing,

D7 G   D7   G
"Glory to the newborn King!"

Verse 3

```
         G                           D7
Hail, the heav'n-born Prince of peace!

G     C    D7     G
Hail, the Son of Righteousness!

              Em    A7
Light and life to all He brings,

D                 A7   D
Ris'n with healing in his wings.

G            C    D7
Mild He lays His glory by,

G            C          D7
Born that man no more may die,

C     E7    Am
Born to raise the sons of earth,

D7    G         D7    G
Born to give them second birth.

C     E7    Am
Hark! the herald angels sing,

D7    G    D7     G
"Glory to the newborn King!"
```

Hear Them Bells

Words and Music by
D.S. McCosh

Melody:

Hear them bells,... _____

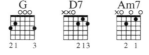

G   D7   Am7

Verse

G
Hear them bells,

D7   G
Merry Christmas bells!

  Am7
They are ringing out the

D7   G
Evil of the sword.

Hear them bells,

D7   G
Merry Christmas bells!

  Am7
They are ringing in the

D7   G
Glory of the Lord!

He Is Born

Traditional French Carol

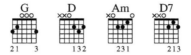

| G | D | Am | D7 |
| 21 3 | 1 3 2 | 2 3 1 | 2 1 3 |

Chorus 1

G
He is born, the holy Child,

D
Play the oboe and bagpipes merrily.

G
He is born, the holy Child,

D　**G**
Sing we all of the Savior mild.

Verse 1

  G   D G
Through long ages of the past,

             D
Prophets have betold His coming,

 G   D G
Through long ages of the past;

         Am G D7
Now the time has come at last!

Chorus 2 Repeat Chorus 1

Verse 2

  G   D G
O how lovely, O how pure

             D
Is this perfect Child of heaven;

 G   D G
O how lovely, O how pure,

         Am G D7
Gracious gift of God to man!

Chorus 3 Repeat Chorus 1

Hear, O Shepherds

Traditional Croation Carol

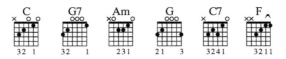

Verse

    C   **G7**   **C**
Hear, O shepherds, hear while I tell you,

  G7 **C**   **G7**   **C**
Hark to the miracle that only now befell you:

   Am   **G**   **C**   **G** **C7**
On a manger lowly, in a prickly stall____

F   **G** **Am** **C**   **G**   **C** **C7**
Lies the baby ho - ly____ who will save us all.____

F   **G** **Am** **C**   **G7**   **C**
Lies the baby ho - ly____ who will save us all.

How Brightly Beams the Morning Star

Words and Music by Philipp Nicolai
Translated by William Mercer
Harmonized by J.S. Bach

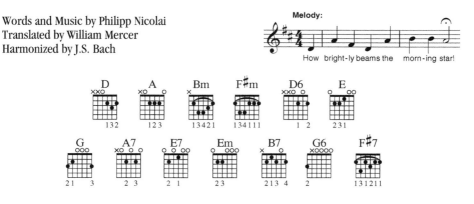

Verse 1

D   A   D Bm   F#m D6 E   A
How brightly beams the__ morning star!

D   G   A7 D   E7 A   D6 E7 A
What sud-den rad - i - ance from a - far

D   G   D Em D A7   D
Doth glad us with its shin - ing?

    A D Bm F#m D6   E A
The ray of God that__ breaks our night

D   G   A7 D E7 A D6   E7   A
And fills the dark - ened souls with light,

D   G   D Em D   A7   D
Who long for truth were pin - ing.

A   D   A Bm Em D A7   D
Thy word, Je - sus, tru - ly feeds us,

A7 D A   B7
Rightly leads us,

Em Bm   G6 A7 D
Life be - stow - ing.

Bm   F#7 G   D   G   D G6 A7 D
Praise, oh__ praise such love o'erflow - ing.

Verse 2

```
D      A    D  Bm F#m D6   E  A
```
Through Thee a - lone can we__ be blest;

```
D    G    A7 D E7  A  D6   E7 A
```
Then deep be on__ our hearts im-prest

```
D  G   D   Em  D  A7    D
```
The love that Thou hast borne us;

```
   A   D  Bm   F#m  D6 E   A
```
So make us read - y____ to ful - fill

```
D   G   A7 D  E7   A  D6 E7 A
```
With burning seal____ Thy ho - ly will,

```
D     G   D   Em D A7   D
```
Though men may vex or scorn us;

```
A  D   A  Bm  Em  D A7  D
```
Savior, let us__ nev - er lose Thee,

```
A7 D  A      B7
```
For we choose Thee,

```
Em   Bm   G6  A7  D
```
Thirst to__ know__ Thee,

```
Bm F#7  G   D   G   D  G6 A7  D
```
All are__ we and have we owe__ Thee!

Verse 3

```
           A     D  Bm F#m D6   E  A
O praise to Him who came to save,

D   G   A7   D E7  A   D6   E7 A
Who conquer'd death and burst the grave;

D   G   D   Em   D  A7   D
Each day new praise re - soundeth

   A   D  Bm  F#m D6   E   A
To Him the Lamb who once was slain,

D  G     A7 D E7    A   D6  E7 A
The Friend who none__ shall trust in vain,

D    G     D  Em  D  A7   D
Whose grace for ay__ a - boundeth;

A    D A   Bm Em D  A7  D
Sing, ye heavens, tell the sto - ry

A7 D   A    B7
Of His glo - ry,

Em Bm    G6  A7   D
Till His__ prais - es

Bm  F#m G    D    G  D  G6 A7 D
Flood with light earth's darkest plac - es!
```

The Holly and the Ivy

18th Century English Carol

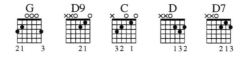

Verse 1

      G   **D9 G**
The holly and the ivy,

C G   **C D**
When they are both full grown,

 G   **C D**
Of all the trees that are in the wood,

C G   **D7 G**
The holly bears the crown.

Chorus 1

C G   **D9 G**
The rising of the sun

C G   **C D**
And the running of the deer,

 G   **C   D C**
The playing of the merry or - gan,

   G   **D7 G**
Sweet singing in the choir.

Verse 2

     G   **D9 G**
The holly bears a___ blossom

C G   **C D**
As white as li - ly flow'r,

 G   **C**   **D**
And Mary bore sweet Jesus Christ

C G   **D7 G**
To be our dear Sav - ior.

Chorus 2	Repeat Chorus 1

Verse 3

      G   **D9** **G**
The holly bears a__ berry

C G   **C D**
As red as an - y blood,

      G   **C**   **D**
And Mary bore sweet Jesus Christ

C G   **D7** **G**
To do poor sinners good.

Chorus 3	Repeat Chorus 1

Verse 4

      G   **D9** **G**
The holly bears a__ prickle

C G   **C D**
As sharp as an - y thorn,

      G   **C**   **D**
And Mary bore sweet Jesus Christ

C G   **D7** **G**
On Christmas day in the morn.

Chorus 4	Repeat Chorus 1

Verse 5

      G   **D9** **G**
The holly bears a__ bark

C G   **C D**
As bitter as the gall,

      G   **C**   **D**
And Mary bore sweet Jesus Christ

C G   **D7 G**
For to redeem us all.

Chorus 5	Repeat Chorus 1
Verse 6	Repeat Verse 1
Chorus 6	Repeat Chorus 1

I Go to Bethlehem

Traditional Czech Carol

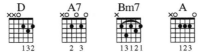

Verse 1

> **D   A7**
> I go to Bethlehem,
>
> **D   A7**
> To see the tiny child;
>
> **D   A7**
> My black rooster, trim and sleek,
>
> **Bm7   A**
> My cuckoo with song so sweet:
>
> **D   A7   D**
> These will I give Him.

Verse 2

    D   A7
Rooster will crow away

    D   A7
Making the Baby gay;

    D   A7
Cuckoo perching near His little head,

    Bm7   A
Calling, softly will make His heart glad:

    D   A7 D
These will I give Him.

Outro

    D
Coo, coo-coo!

Coo, coo-coo!

      A7 D   A7 D
Jesus, He sings for you!

Coo, coo-coo!

Coo, coo-coo!

      A7 D   A7 D
Jesus, He sings for you!

I Heard the Bells on Christmas Day

Words by Henry Wadsworth Longfellow
Music by John Baptiste Calkin

Melody:

I heard the bells on Christ-mas day,...

G   C   D7   Em   F#   Bm   Am   E7

Verse 1

G   C   D7
I heard the bells on Christmas day,

  Em   F# Bm
Their old familiar carols play,

  Am   D7   Bm   E7
And mild and sweet the words re-peat,

  Am   E7   Em D7
Of peace on earth, goodwill to men.

Verse 2

G   C   D7
I thought how as the day had come,

  Em   F# Bm
The belfries of all Christendom

  Am   D7   Bm E7
Had rolled a - long th'un - broken song

  Am   E7   D7 G
Of peace on earth, goodwill to men.

                        G   C   D7
Verse 3   And in despair I bowed my head:

                        Em   F#   Bm
                "There is no peace on earth," I said,

                        Am   D7   Bm   E7
                "For hate is strong, and mocks the song

                        Am   E7   Em   D7
                Of peace on earth, goodwill to men."

                        G   C   D7
Verse 4   Then pealed the bells more loud and deep:

                        Em   F#   Bm
                "God is not dead, nor doth He sleep;

                        Am   D7   Bm   E7
                The wrong shall fail, the right pre - vail,

                        Am   E7   D7   G
                With peace on earth, goodwill to men."

                        G   C   D7
Verse 5   Till ringing, singing on its way,

                        Em   F#   Bm
                The world revolved from night to day,

                        Am   D7   Bm   E7
                A voice, a chime, a chant sublime,

                        Am   E7   D7   G
                Of peace on earth, goodwill to men!

I Saw Three Ships

Traditional English Carol

Verse 1

      G   D   G   D
I saw three ships come sailing in

      G   D
On Christmas day, on Christmas day;

      G   D   G   D
I saw three ships come sailing in

      G   D G
On Christmas day in the morning.

Verse 2

      G   D   G   D
And what was in those ships all three

      G   D
On Christmas day, on Christmas day?

      G   D   G   D
And what was in those ships all three

      G   D G
On Christmas day in the morning?

GUITAR CHORD SONGBOOK

Verse 3

    G   D   G   D
Our Savior Christ and His la - dy

    G   D
On Christmas day, on Christmas day.

    G   D   G   D
Our Savior Christ and His la - dy

    G   D   G
On Christmas day in the morning.

Verse 4

    G   D   G   D
Pray, whither sailed those ships all three

    G   D
On Christmas day, on Christmas day?

    G   D   G   D
Pray, whither sailed those ships all three

    G   D   G
On Christmas day, on Christmas day?

Verse 5

    G   D G   D
O, they sailed into Bethlehem

    G   D
On Christmas day, on Christmas day;

    G   D G   D
O, they sailed into Bethlehem

    G   D   G
On Christmas day in the morning.

Verse 6

    G   D   G   D
And all the bells on earth shall ring

    G   D
On Christmas day, on Christmas day;

    G   D   G   D
And all the bells on earth shall ring

    G   D   G
On Christmas day in the morning.

Verse 7

```
    G    D    G        D
And all the angels in heav'n shall sing
    G              D
On Christmas day, on Christmas day;
    G    D    G        D
And all the angels in heav'n shall sing
    G              D  G
On Christmas day in the morning.
```

Verse 8

```
    G    D    G        D
And all the souls on earth shall sing
    G              D
On Christmas day, on Christmas day;
    G    D    G        D
And all the souls on earth shall sing
    G              D  G
On Christmas day in the morning.
```

Verse 9

```
    G    D    G        D
Then let us all re - joice a - main
    G              D
On Christmas day, on Christmas day;
    G    D    G    D
Then let us all re - joice a - main
    G              D  G
On Christmas day in the morning!
```

Infant So Gentle

Traditional French Carol

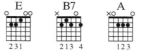

```
  E          B7          A
o   oo     x    o      xo     o

2 3 1      2 1 3  4     1 2 3
```

Verse 1

    E   B7 E   A   E B7 E
Infant so gentle, so pure and so sweet;

          B7 E   A E B7 E
Love from Thy tiny eyes sinners doth greet.

B7   E A E B7   E
Tend'rest words fail all Thy beauty to show;

        B7 E   A   E A E B7   E
We must a - dore Thee, if Thee we would know.

Verse 2

    E   B7 E   A   E B7 E
Infant so holy, so meak and so mild,

         B7 E   A E B7   E
We come to welcome Thee, our dear Christ child.

B7   E A E B7   E
We cannot tell Thee how much we do need,

       B7 E A   E A E B7 E
Thy precious presence; all sinners take heed.

Infant Holy, Infant Lowly

Traditional Polish Carol
Paraphrased by Edith M.G. Reed

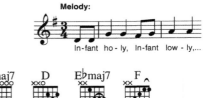

G   D7   C   F#°7   Cmaj7   D   E♭maj7   F

Verse 1

          G   **D7**
Infant holy, Infant lowly,

          G   **D7** **G**
For His bed a cattle stall.

                  D7
Oxen lowing, little knowing

          G   **D7**   **G**
Christ the Babe is Lord of all.

            C   **F#°7**
Swift are winging angels singing,

          Cmaj7   **D**
Noels ringing, tidings bringing:

          G   **D7**   **G**
Christ the Babe is Lord of all.

```
| Ebmaj7        | F        | G
```

Verse 2

```
                    G                    D7
```
Flocks are sleeping, shepherds keeping

```
          G     D7      G
```
Vigil till the morning new,

```
                          D7
```
Saw the glory, heard the story,

```
          G   D7    G
```
Tidings of a Gospel true.

```
              C                 F#°7
```
Thus re - joicing, free from sorrow,

```
          Cmaj7           D
```
Praises voicing greet the morrow:

```
          G       D7      G
```
Christ the Babe was born for you.

Irish Carol

Traditional Irish Carol

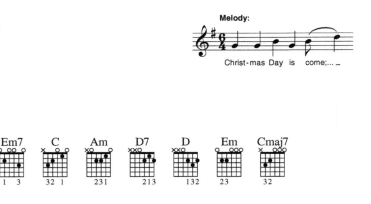

Verse 1

    G   Em7   C   G   Am
Christmas Day is come; let's all pre-pare for mirth,

D7 G   Em7   C D Em Am G
Which fills the heav'ns and earth at this a - maz - ing birth.

D   G   Em7   C   G   Am
Through both the joyous angels in strife and hurry fly,

D7 G   Em7   C   D Em Am G
With glory and ho-sannas, "All Ho - ly" do they cry,

D7 G   C   D   G   C   D
In_ heav'n the church tri-umphant a-dores with all her choirs,

    Em   Cmaj7   D Em7 C   D7 G
The militant on earth with hum-ble faith ad-mires.

Verse 2

```
          G            Em7       C     G     Am
But why should we re-joice? Should we not rather mourn

D7 G          Em7       C D Em  Am G
To see the hope of nations thus in a  sta - ble born?

D      G           Em7          C     G          Am
Where are His crown and scepter, where is His throne sub-lime,

D7   G            Em7       C     D Em  Am   G
Where is His throne ma-jestic that should the stars out - shine?

D7 G      C          D          G   C      D
Is_ there no sumptuous palace, nor any inn at all

   Em              Cmaj7      D   Em7 C   D7 G
To lodge His heav'nly mother but in_ a_   filth-y   stall?
```

Verse 3

```
          G            Em7       C      G     Am
Oh! Cease, ye blessed angels, such clam'rous joys to make!

D7    G            Em7      C     D   Em Am   G
Though midnight silence favors, the shep-herds are a  -  wake;

D  G          Em7    C      G        Am
And you, o glorious star, that with new splendor brings,

D7   G          Em7      C    D  Em  Am G
From the remotest parts three learned east - ern kings,

D7   G       C        D         G      C       D
Turn somewhere else your luster, your rags else-where dis-play,

   Em              Cmaj7      D   Em7 C    D7 G
For Herod may slay the babe, and Christ must straight a - way.
```

Verse 4

```
          G            Em7     C   G     Am
If we would then re-joice, let's cancel the old score,

D7  G          Em7           C    D Em  Am G
And purposing amendment, re-solve to sin_ no_ more;

D  G            Em7          C   G           Am
For mirth can ne'er content us, with-out a conscience clear;

D7 G             Em7        C  D  Em Am G
And thus we'll find true pleasure in all the u - sual cheer,

D7   G     C        D         G       C       D
In__ dancing, sporting, rev'ling, with masquerade and drum,

   Em         Cmaj7  D   Em7 C   D7 G
So Christmas merry be,_ as Chris-tians doth be - come.
```

It Came Upon the Midnight Clear

Words by Edmund H. Sears
Traditional English Melody
Adapted by Arthur Sullivan

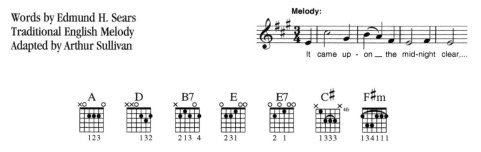

A   D   B7   E   E7   C#   F#m

Verse 1

    A   **D** **A**
It came up - on the midnight clear,

  D   **B7**   **E** **E7**
That glorious song of old,___

    A   **D**   **A**
From angels bending near the earth

  D   **E**   **A**
To touch their harps of gold:

    C#   **F#m**
"Peace on the earth, good-will to men,

    E   **B7**   **E** **E7**
From heav'n's all-gracious King."___

    A   **D**   **A**
The world in solemn stillness lay

  D   **E7** **A**
To hear the angels sing.

Verse 2

      A   D   A
Still through the cloven skies they came

     D   B7   E   E7
With peaceful wings un-furled,___

     A   D   A
And still their heavenly music floats

     D   E   A
O'er all the weary world;

  C#   F#m
A-bove its sad and lowly plains,

     E   B7   E   E7
They bend on hovering wing.___

     A   D   A
And ever o'er its Babel sounds

     D   E7   A
The blessed angels sing.

Verse 3

     A   D   A
And ye, be-neath life's crushing load,

      D   B7   E E7
Whose forms are bending low,___

     A   D   A
Who toil a-long the climbing way

     D   E   A
With painful steps and slow,

   C#   F#m
Look now! For glad and golden hours

      E   B7   E   E7
Come swiftly on the wing.___

     A   D   A
O rest be-side the weary road,

     D   E7   A
And hear the angels sing.

Verse 4

    A   **D**   **A**
For lo! The days are hastening on,

    D   **B7**   **E** **E7**
By prophet seen of old,___

     A   **D** **A**
When, with the ever-circling years,

     D   **E**   **A**
Shall come the time fore-told

      C#   **F#m**
When peace shall over all the earth

    E   **B7**   **E** **E7**
Its ancient splendors fling,___

    A   **D**   **A**
And the whole world send back the song

     D   **E7** **A**
Which now the angels sing.

Jingle Bells

Words and Music by
J. Pierpont

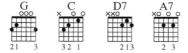

Verse 1

   G
Dashing through the snow,

         C
In a one-horse open sleigh,

       D7
O'er the fields we go,

       G
Laughing all the way.

Bells on bobtail ring,

      C
Making spirits bright,

        G
What fun it is to ride and sing

D7   **G**
A sleighing song to-night! Oh!

Chorus 1

G
Jingle bells, jingle bells,

Jingle all the way.

C   **G**
Oh what fun it is to ride

  A7   **D7**
In a one-horse open sleigh!

G
Jingle bells, jingle bells,

Jingle all the way.

C   **G**
Oh what fun it is to ride

 D7   **G**
In a one-horse open sleigh!

Verse 2

  G
A day or two ago

     C
I thought I'd take a ride,

      D7
And soon Miss Fanny Bright

    G
Was seated by my side.

The horse was lean and lank,

      C
Misfortune seemed his lot,

    G
He got into a drifted bank

  D7 **G**
And we, we got up-shot! Oh!

Chorus 2   Repeat Chorus 1

                     G

Verse 3   Now the ground is white,

                             C

Go it while you're young.

                             D7

And take the girls to-night

                            G

And sing this sleighing song.

Just get a bobtail bay,

                        C

Two-forty for his speed,

                          G

Then hitch him to an open sleigh

    D7   **G**

And crack, you'll take the lead! Oh!

Chorus 3   Repeat Chorus 1

Jolly Old St. Nicholas

Traditional 19th Century American Carol

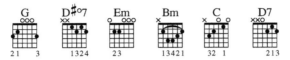

Verse 1

G   D#°7
Jolly old Saint Nicholas,

Em   Bm
Lean your ear this way.

C   G
Don't you tell a single soul

D7
What I'm going to say.

G   D#°7
Christmas Eve is coming soon,

Em   Bm
Now, you dear old man,

C   G
Whisper what you'll bring to me;

D7   G
Tell me if you can.

Verse 2

```
G                   D#°7
When the clock is striking twelve,

Em          Bm
When I'm fast a-sleep,

C           G
Down the chimney broad and black,

D7
With your pack you'll creep.

G                   D#°7
All the stockings you will find

Em          Bm
Hanging in a row.

C           G
Mine will be the shortest one,

D7              G
You'll be sure to know.
```

Verse 3

```
G           D#°7
Johnny wants a pair of skates;

Em          Bm
Susy wants a sled;

C           G
Nellie wants a picture book,

D7
Yellow, blue, and red;

G           D#°7
Now I think I'll leave to you

Em          Bm
What to give the rest.

C               G
Choose for me, dear Santa Claus,

D7              G
You will know the best.
```

Joseph Dearest, Joseph Mine

Traditional German Carol

Jo - seph dear - est, Jo - seph mine,...

Verse 1

```
         G                C   G
Joseph dearest, Jo-seph mine,
                       C   G
Help me cradle the Babe di-vine,
Am          D7   Am  G   D
Sing to Him a__ lull - a - by:
        G
"Now sleep and rest,
       C        D
Your slumber blest,
    G
O Jesus."
```

Chorus 1

```
        G       D       Em      Cmaj7
He came a-mong us at Christmas time,

G  Em      Cmaj7 G A7sus4 A    D
At Christmas time__ in Beth - le - hem,

G     D   G C   D  D7 G
Bringing all men far and wide

C     D    D7 G
Love's Di - a - dem.

D    G Bm Em
Ei - a, ei - a.

C     G        C      D7      G
Jesus Christ, who came to earth to save us.
```

Verse 2

```
G               C G
Gladly, Mother Mary mine,

                C G
Will I rock the Babe divine,

Am        D7 Am G  D
While I sing a__ lull - a - by:

    G
"O sleep and rest,

        C      D
Your slumber blest,

    G
O Jesus!"
```

Chorus 2   Repeat Chorus 1

CHRISTMAS CAROLS   **89**

Joy to the World

Words by Isaac Watts
Music by George Frideric Handel
Arranged by Lowell Mason

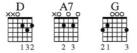

Verse 1

    D   **A7 D**
Joy to the world! The Lord is_ come;

    G   **A7**   **D**
Let earth re-ceive her King;

Let ev'ry heart prepare Him room,

And heav'n and nature sing,

    A7
And heav'n and nature sing,

    D   **A7** **D**
And heav'n and heav'n and na-ture sing.

Verse 2

    D   **A7 D**
Joy to the earth! The Sav-ior reigns;

    G   **A7**   **D**
Let men their songs em-ploy;

While fields and floods, rocks, hills and plains

Repeat the sounding joy,

    A7
Re-peat the sounding joy,

    D   **A7 D**
Re-peat, repeat the sound-ing joy.

Verse 3

    D   **A7**   **D**
No more let sin and sor-rows grow,

    G   **A7**   **D**
Nor thorns in-fest the ground;

He comes to make His blessings flow

Far as the curse is found,

    A7
Far as the curse is found,

    D   **A7 D**
Far as, far as the curse is_ found.

Verse 4

    D   **A7 D**
He rules the world with truth and grace,

    G   **A7**   **D**
And makes the nations prove

The glories of His righteousness

And wonders of His love,

    A
And wonders of His love,

    D   **A7 D**
And wonders, wonders of His love.

Love Came Down at Christmas

Text by Christina Rossetti
Traditional Irish Melody

Melody:

Love came down at Christ - mas,...

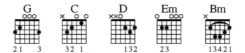

G   C   D   Em   Bm

Verse 1

    G   **C D** **G**
Love came down at Christmas,

          C G   **D**
Love all lovely, love divine;___

Em C   **G** **C G**   **D G**
Love___ was born at Christmas,___

D G   **Bm D** **Em C G**
Star___ and an - gels gave the sign.

Verse 2
```
         G        C  D  G
         Worship we the God-head,

                  C    G       D
         Love incarnate, love divine;__

         Em C   G  C  G   D G
         Wor - ship we our Je - sus,__

         D G       Bm D Em C   G
         But__ wherewith for sa - cred sign?
```

Verse 3
```
         G        C  D  G
         Love shall be our to - ken;

                  C   G        D
         Love be yours and love be mine,__

         Em C   G  C  G   D G
         Love__ to God and neighbor,__

         D  G      Bm D  Em C  G
         Love__ for plea and gift and sign.
```

O Christmas Tree

Traditional German Carol

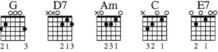

O Christ-mas tree, O Christ-mas tree,...

G	D7	Am	C	E7

Verse 1

    G   **D7 G**
O Christmas tree, O Christmas tree,

      Am   **D7 G**
You stand in verdant beauty!

             D7 G
O Christmas tree, O Christmas tree,

      Am   **D7 G**
You stand in verdant beauty!

           C   **D7**
Your boughs are green in summer's glow,

           G
And do not fade in winter's snow.

D7 G   **D7 G**   **E7**
O_ Christmas tree, O_ Christmas tree,

      Am   **D7 G**
You stand in verdant beauty!

Verse 2

       G   **D7 G**
O Christmas tree, O Christmas tree,

      Am   **D7 G**
Much pleasure doth thou bring me!

            D7 G
O Christmas tree, O Christmas tree,

      Am   **D7 G**
Much pleasure doth thou bring me!

       C   **D7**
For ev'ry year the Christmas tree

            G
Brings to us all both joy and glee.

D7 G   **D7 G**   **E7**
O_ Christmas tree, O_ Christmas tree,

      Am   **D7 G**
Much pleasure doth thou bring me!

Verse 3

       G   **D7 G**
O Christmas tree, O_ Christmas tree,

      Am   **D7 G**
Thy candles shine out brightly!

          D7 G
O Christmas tree, O_ Christmas tree,

      Am   **D7 G**
Thy candles shine out brightly!

           C   **D7**
Each bough doth hold its tiny light

            G
That makes each toy to sparkle bright.

D7 G   **D7 G**   **E7**
O_ Christmas tree, O_ Christmas tree,

      Am   **D7 G**
Thy candles shine out brightly!

O Come, All Ye Faithful
(Adeste Fideles)

Words and Music by John Francis Wade
Latin Words translated by Frederick Oakeley

Melody:

O come, all ye faith - ful,...

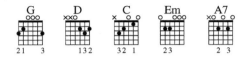

Verse 1

    G   D   G   C   G D
O come all ye faithful, joyful and tri-um-phant,

    Em A7 D   G   D A7 D
O come ye, o come ye to Beth - le - hem.

    G   D   C G D   Em   D
Come and behold Him, born the King of angels.

Chorus 1

    G   D G
O come let us a-dore Him,

         D G D
O come let us a-dore Him,

    C   A7 D C
O come let us a-dore Him,

   G   D   G
Christ___ the Lord.

GUITAR CHORD SONGBOOK

Verse 2

     G   **D**   **G**   **C**   **G D**
Sing choirs of angels, sing in ex - ul - ta - tion,

     Em A7 D G   **D**   **A7**   **D**
Sing, all_ ye citizens of heav-en a - bove.

     G **D**   **C** **G** **D**   **Em**   **D**
Glo-ry to God__ in the high - est.

Chorus 2   Repeat Chorus 1

Verse 3

     G   **D**   **G**   **C**   **G D**
Yea, Lord, we greet Thee, born this happy morning.

     Em A7   **D G**   **D A7**   **D**
Je-sus, to Thee be all glo-ry__ giv'n.

     G **D**   **C G** **D**   **Em**   **D**
Word of the Father, now in flesh ap-pearing.

Chorus 3   Repeat Chorus 1

O Come, Little Children

Words by C. von Schmidt
Music by J.P.A. Schulz

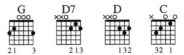

G	D7	D	C

Verse 1

    G   D7   G
O come, little children, from cot and from hall,

                  D7   G
O come to the manger in Bethlehem's stall.

      D   D7   G   C
There meekly He lieth, the heavenly Child,

      D   G   D7   G
So poor and so humble, so sweet and so mild.

Verse 2

    G   D7   G
Now "Glory to God" sing the angels on high,

                       D7   G
And "Peace upon earth" heav'nly voices re-ply.

      D   D7   G   C
Then come, little children, and join in the day

      D   G   D7   G
That gladdened the world on that first Christmas day.

O Little Town of Bethlehem

Words by Phillips Brooks
Music by Lewis H. Redner

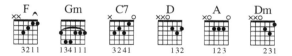

F	Gm	C7	D	A	Dm
xx		x	xxo	xo o	xxo
3211	134111	3241	132	123	231

Verse 1

        F   Gm
O little town of Bethlehem,

        C7   F
How still we see thee lie!

         D   Gm
Above thy deep and dreamless sleep

        C7   F
The silent stars go by.

        C7   A
Yet in thy dark streets shineth

    Dm   A
The everlasting light.

      F   Gm
The hopes and fears of all the years

    C7   F
Are met in thee to-night.

Verse 2

```
        F            Gm
For Christ is born of Mary,

        C7           F
And gathered all a-bove,

               D     Gm
While mortals sleep, the angels keep

        C7                F
Their watch of wond'ring love.

              C7      A
O morning stars, to-gether

        Dm          A
Pro-claim the holy birth!

        F            Gm
And praises sing to God the King,

        C7           F
And peace to men on earth!
```


Verse 3

```
        F            Gm
How silently, how silently

        C7           F
The wondrous gift is giv'n!

              D     Gm
So God im-parts to human hearts

        C7           F
The blessings of His heav'n.

              C7      A
No ear may hear His coming,

        Dm          A
But in this world of sin,

        F               Gm
Where meek souls will re-ceive Him still,

        C7              F
The dear Christ enters in.
```

	F Gm
Verse 4	O holy Child of Bethlehem,
	C7 F
	De-scend to us, we pray;
	D Gm
	Cast out our sin and enter in;
	C7 F
	Be born in us to-day.
	C7 A
	We hear the Christmas angels
	Dm A
	The great glad tidings tell;
	F Gm
	O come to us, a-bide with us,
	C7 F
	Our Lord Em-man-u-el!

O Come, O Come Emmanuel

Plainsong, 13th Century
Words translated by John M. Neale
and Henry S. Coffin

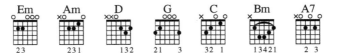

Em   Am   D   G   C   Bm   A7

Verse 1

       Em   Am   D   G
O come, O come, Em - man - u - el,

       Em   C   Am Bm Em
And ransom captive Is - ra - el,

         Am   Em A7   D
That mourns in lonely ex - ile here

       Em   Am D   G
Un-til the Son of God__ ap-pear.

Chorus 1

        D   Em
Re-joice, re-joice!

        C   D   Em   G   C   Am   Bm Em
Em - man - u - el shall come to Thee, O Is - ra - el!

Verse 2

       Em   Am D   G
O come, Thou Dayspring, come__and cheer

       Em   C   Am Bm   Em
Our spirits by Thine ad - vent here;

        Am   Em A7   D
Dis-perse the gloomy clouds__ of night,

       Em   Am D   G
And death's dark shadows put___ to flight.

GUITAR CHORD SONGBOOK

Chorus 2   Repeat Chorus 1

              Em   Am D   G
Verse 3   O come, Thou Wisdom, from__ on high,

                 Em C   Am Bm   Em
         And order all things far____ and nigh;

                 Am   Em A7   D
         To us the path of know - ledge show,

                 Em   Am D   G
         And cause us in her ways__ to go.

Chorus 3   Repeat Chorus 1

              Em   Am D   G
Verse 4   O come, desire of na - tions, bind

                 Em C   Am Bm   Em
         All people in one heart__ and mind;

                 Am   Em Am   D
         Bid envy, strife, and quar - rels cease;

                 Em   Am D   G
         Fill the whole world with heav - en's peace.

Chorus 4   Repeat Chorus 1

              Em   Am D   G
Verse 5   O come, Thou Key of Da - vid, come,

                 Em C   Am Bm   Em
         And open wide our heav - 'nly home.

                 Am   Em A7
         Make safe the way that leads__ on high,

                 Em   Am D   G
         And close the path to mis - er - y.

Chorus 5   Repeat Chorus 1

O Holy Night

French Words by Placide Cappeau
English Words by John S. Dwight
Music by Adolphe Adam

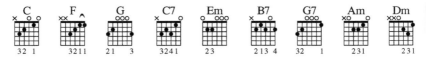

Verse 1

    C   F   C
O holy night, the stars are brightly shining,

                 G   C
It is the night of the dear Savior's birth;

                     F   C C7
Long lay the world in sin and error pin - ing,

             Em   B7   Em
Till He ap-peared and the soul felt its worth.

  G7   C
A thrill of hope, the weary world rejoices,

    G7   C
For yonder breaks a new and glorious morn;

Am   Em   Dm   Am
Fall on your knees! O, hear the angel voices!

   C G7   C F   C G7   C
O night__ di-vine,__ O night__ when Christ was born!

   G G7   C F C G7   C
O night,__ O ho - ly night, O night di-vine!

Verse 2

         C   F   C
Truly He taught us to love one an-other,

                         G   C
His law is love, and His gospel is peace;

                                F   C   C7
Chains shall He break, for the slave is our broth-er,

            Em   B7   Em
And in His name all op-pression shall cease.

        G7   C
Sweet hymns of joy in grateful chorus raise we,

        G7   C
Let all within us praise His holy name;

Am   Em   Dm   Am
Christ is the Lord, O praise His name for-ever!

     C G7   C F   C G7   C
His pow'r__ and glo - ry ev - er more pro-claim!

     G G7   C F   C G7   C
His pow'r__ and glo - ry ev - er more pro-claim!

Once in Royal David's City

Words by Cecil F. Alexander
Music by Henry J. Gauntlett

Melody:

Once in roy - al Da - vid's _ cit - y...

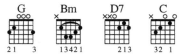

G   Bm   D7   C

Verse 1

   G
Once in royal David's city

     Bm   **D7**   **G**
Stood a lowly cattle shed,

Where a mother laid her Baby

     Bm   **D7**   **G**
In a manger for His bed.

C   **G**   **D7**   **G**
Mary was that mother mild,

C   **G**   **D7** **G**
Jesus Christ her little Child.

Verse 2

   G
He came down to earth from heaven,

     Bm   **D7**   **G**
Who is God and Lord of all,

And His shelter was a stable,

     Bm   **D7**   **G**
And His cradle was a stall.

C   **G**   **D7**   **G**
With the poor, and mean, and lowly,

C   **G**   **D7**   **G**
Lived on earth our Savior holy.

Verse 3

G
Jesus is our childhood's pattern,

Bm   D7   G
Day by day like us He grew;

He was little, weak and helpless,

Bm   D7   G
Tears and smiles like us He knew.

C   G   D7   G
And He feeleth for our sadness,

C   G   D7   G
And He shareth in our gladness.

Verse 4

G
And our eyes at last shall see Him,

Bm   D7   G
Through His own re-deeming love,

For that child so dear and gentle

Bm   D7   G
Is our Lord in heav'n a-bove.

C   G   D7   G
And He leads His children on

C   G   D7 G
To the place where He is gone.

Pat-A-Pan
(Willie, Take Your Little Drum)

Words and Music by
Bernard de la Monnoye

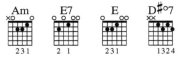

Am	E7	E	D#°7
2 3 1	2 1	2 3 1	1 3 2 4

Verse 1

      Am   **E7** **Am**
Willie, take your little drum,

     E7   **E**   **D#°7** **E**
Robin, bring your whis - tle,___ come.

               Am
When we hear the fife and drum,

              E
Tu-re-lu-re-lu, pat-a-pat-a-pan.

               Am
When we hear the fife and drum,

       E7   **Am** **E** **Am**
Christmas should be light and fun.

Verse 2

      Am   **E7**   **Am**
Thus the men of olden days

      E7   **E**   **D#°7 E**
Gave the King of Kings their praise.

             Am
When they hear the fife and drum,

             E
Tu-re-lu-re-lu, pat-a-pat-a-pan.

             Am
With the drums they sing and play,

   E7   **Am**   **E**   **Am**
Full of joy on Christ-mas day.

Verse 3

      Am   **E7**   **Am**
God and man are now be-come

      E7   **E** **D#°7**   **E**
Closely joined as fife and__ drum.

             Am
When we play the fife and drum,

             E
Tu-re-lu-re-lu, pat-a-pat-a-pan.

             Am
When on fife and drum we play,

   E7   **Am** **E** **Am**
Dance and make the hol - i - day.

Rejoice and Be Merry

Gallery Carol

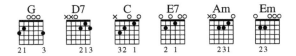

Verse

   G   D7 G   D7
Re-joice and be merry in songs and in mirth!

G C   G   C D7 G
O praise our Re-deemer, all mor - tals on earth!

      D7   E7   Am
For this is the birthday of Jesus our King,

D7 Em   D7   G C D7 G
Who brought us sal-vation His prais - es we'll sing!

Rocking

Traditional Czech Carol

Melody:

Ba - by Je - sus, gen - tly __ sleep,...

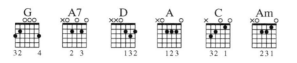

Verse 1

G		A7	D	A	D

Baby Jesus, gently sleep, do not stir;

C   G   D   G
We will bring a coat of fur.

       C   D
We will rock you, rock you, rock you,

G   C   Am   D
Gently slumber as we rock you,

G   A7   D
See the fur to keep you warm,

C   G   D G
Snugly fits your tiny form.

Verse 2

G   A7 D A   D
Mary's precious baby sleep, gently sleep,

C   G   D   G
Sleep in comfort, slumber deep.

       C   D
We will rock you, rock you, rock you,

G   C   Am   D
Gently slumber as we rock you,

G   A7   D
We will praise you all we can,

C   G   D G
Darling, darling little man.

Ring Out, Ye Wild and Merry Bells

Words and Music by
C. Maitland

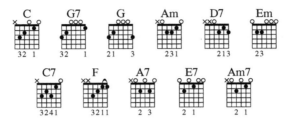

Verse 1

      C   G7   C   G7
Ring out, ye wild and merry bells,

      C   **G7 C**
Ring out the old, old sto - ry

      G7   C   G7
That first was told by angel tongues

    G   Am   D7 G
From out the realms of glo - ry.

Em
Peace on earth was their sweet song,

     D7 G7
Glory in the high-est!

C7   **F A7 D7 G7**
Echoing all the hills away,

E7   Am7 D7 G7   C
Glory in__ the high-est!

Chorus 1

F   C7   F

Ring, sweet bells, ring ever-more,

             C7   F

Peal from ev'ry stee - ple.

D7   G7   E7   Am

Christ, the Lord, shall be our God

    C   Am   G7 C

And we shall be His peo - ple!

Verse 2

    C   G7   C   G7

Ring out, ye silv'ry bells, ring out,

    C   G7 C

Ring out your exul-ta - tion

        G7   C   G7

That God with man is recon-ciled.

     Am   D7 G

Go tell it to the na - tions.

Em

Therefore let us all today,

      D7   G7

Glory in the high-est!

C7   F   A7 D7 G7

Banish sor - row far a-way,

E7   Am7 D7 G7   C

Glory in__ the high - est!

Chorus 2   Repeat Chorus 1

Rise Up, Shepherd, and Follow

African-American Spiritual

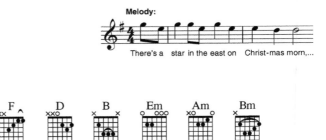

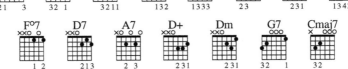

Verse 1

         G
There's a star in the east on Christmas morn,

C   **F**   **D**
Rise up, shepherd, and follow.

       G   **B**
It will lead to the place where the Savior's born,

Em   **Am**   **G**
Rise up, shepherd, and follow.

	Em Bm C G

Chorus 1

Em   Bm   C   G
Leave your ewes and leave your lambs,

D   F°7   D7
Rise up, shepherd, and follow.

Em   Bm   C   G
Leave your sheep and leave your rams,

A7   Am   G
Rise up, shepherd, and follow.

**   D+ D7**
Follow, fol - low,

Dm   D+
Rise up, shepherd, and follow.

G   G7   Cmaj7
Follow the star of Beth-le-hem,__

A7   Am   G   D
Rise up, shepherd, and fol - low.

Verse 2

**   G**
If you take good heed to the angel's word,

C   F   D
Rise up, shepherd, and follow.

**   G   B**
You'll for-get all your flocks, you'll forget your herd,

Em   Am   G
Rise up, shepherd, and follow.

Verse 2   Repeat Chorus 1

Silent Night

Words by Joseph Mohr
Translated by John F. Young
Music by Franz X. Gruber

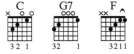

Verse 1

C
Silent night, holy night!

G7   **C**
All is calm, all is bright.

F   **C**
Round yon Virgin Mother and Child.

F   **C**
Holy Infant so tender and mild,

G7   **C**
Sleep in heavenly peace,

    G7   **C**
Sleep in heavenly peace.

Verse 2

C
Silent night, holy night!

G7   C
Shepherds quake at the sight.

F   C
Glories stream from heaven afar,

F   C
Heavenly hosts sing Alleluia,

G7   C
Christ the Savior is born!

          G7   C
Christ the Savior is born.

Verse 3

C
Silent night, holy night!

G7   C
Son of God, love's pure light.

F   C
Radiant beams from Thy holy face

F   C
With the dawn of re-deeming grace,

G7   C
Jesus Lord at Thy birth.

          G7   C
Jesus Lord at Thy birth.

The Sleep of the Infant Jesus

Traditional French Carol

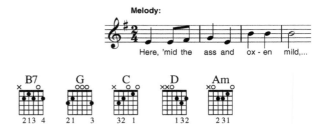

Melody:

Here, 'mid the   ass and   ox - en   mild,...

Em   B   B7   G   C   D   Am

23   1333   213 4   21   3   32 1   1 32   2 31

Verse 1

    Em   **B Em B7**
    Here, 'mid the ass and ox - en mild,

    Em G   C   B
    Sleep, sleep, sleep, thou tiny Child.

    Em   D G   C
    Thousand cheru-bim, thousand sera-phim,

                   Em   Am B7 Em
    Guarding o'er the bed of the great Lord of love.

Verse 2

    Em   **B Em B7**
    Here, 'mid the rose and lil - y bright,

    Em G   C   B
    Sleep, sleep, sleep, thou tiny Child.

    Em   **B Em B7**
    Here, 'mid the shepherds' glad de - light,

    Em G   C   B
    Sleep, sleep, sleep, thou tiny Child.

    Em   D G   C
    Thousand cheru-bim, thousand sera-phim,

                   Em   Am B7 Em
    Guarding o'er the bed of the great Lord of love.

Today We Welcome a Tiny Child

Traditional 14th Century Dutch Carol

G   D   C   D7   Am   Bm   Cadd9

Verse 1

      G   D   G   C   G D7 G
To-day we welcome a_ ti-ny Child

                      D   G
That pales the sun's bright shin - ing,

      D   Am G   D   Bm
Our hope and joy, this Infant mild,

G   Cadd9   G   D7   G
Whom angels' songs are pro-claim-ing.

Verse 2

      G   D   G   C   G   D7 G
The stars that fill the ra - di - ant sky

                      D   G
Announce the gift from heav - en,

      D   Am   G   D   Bm
While Mary a - dores her holy Child,

G   Cadd9   G   D7   G
That God__ the Father has giv - en.

The Snow Lay on the Ground

Traditional Irish Carol

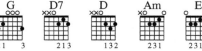

Verse 1

         G   **D7 G   D**
The snow lay on the ground, the star shone bright,

                                  D7 G   D7 G
When Christ our Lord was born on Christmas night.

                   D7 G   D
Venite adoremus Do-mi-num;

                  D7 G D G
Venite adoremus Do-mi-num.

Chorus 1

         G   **Am E Am**
Venite adoremus Do-mi-num;

               D7   G D7 G
Venite adoremus Do-mi-num.

Verse 2

         G   **D7** **G D**
'Twas Mary, Virgin pure, of ho - ly Anne,

                  D7 G   **D7**   **G**
That brought into this world the God made man.

           D7 **G D**
She laid Him in a stall at Beth-le-hem,

           D7 G   **D**   **G**
The ass and oxen share the night with them.

Chorus 2   Repeat Chorus 1

Verse 3

         G   **D7 G** **D**
Saint Joseph, too, was by to tend the Child;

           D7 G   **D7 G**
To guard Him and protect His Moth-er mild;

           D7 **G** **D**
The Angels hovered round and sang this song:

       D7 **G** **D7 G**
Venite adoremus Do-mi-num.

Chorus 3   Repeat Chorus 1

Star of the East

Words by George Cooper
Music by Amanda Kennedy

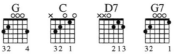

Verse 1

    G   C   G
Star of the East, oh, Bethlehem's star,

                      D7
Guiding us on to heaven a-far!

    G   C   G
Sorrow and grief are lull'd by thy light,

         D7   G   D7   G
Thou hope of each mortal in death's lonely night!

C   G
Fearless and tranquil, we look up to thee,

D7   G   G7
Knowing thou beam'st thro' e-ter-ni-ty!

C   G
Help us to follow where thou still dost guide,

D7   G
Pilgrims of earth so wide.

Verse 2

    G   C   G
Star of the East, thou hope of the soul,

                        D7
While round us here the dark billows roll.

    G   C   G
Lead us from sin to glory a-far,

      D7   G   D7   G
Thou star of the East, thou sweet Bethl'em's star.

              D7   G C G
Oh star that leads to God a - bove,

          D7   G   D7
Whose rays are peace and joy and love.

        G   D7   G C   G
Watch o'er us still 'til life hath ceased.

        D7   G   D7   G
Beam on, bright star, sweet Bethlehem star!

Still, Still, Still

Salzburg Melody, c.1819
Traditional Austrian Text

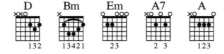

D	Bm	Em	A7	A
132	13421	23	2 3	123

Verse 1

   D   **Bm**
Still, still, still,

    Em   **A7**   **D**
To sleep is now His will.

    A   **D**
On Mary's breast He rests in slumber

  A   **D**
While we pray in endless number.

      Bm
Still, still, still,

    Em   **A7**   **D**
To sleep is now His will.

                              D   **Bm**
Verse 2   Sleep, sleep, sleep,

                              Em   **A7 D**
                  While we Thy vigil keep.

                              A   **D**
                  And angels come from heaven singing

                  A   **D**
                  Songs of jubi-lation bringing

                              Bm
                  Sleep, sleep, sleep,

                              Em   **A7 D**
                  While we Thy vigil keep.

                              Bm
                  Sleep, sleep, sleep,

                              Em   **A7 D**
                  While we Thy vigil keep.

There's a Song in the Air

Words and Music by Josiah G. Holland
and Karl P. Harrington

A   E7   E   B7   A7   D   Dm

A	E7	E	B7	A7	D	Dm
xo o	o o oo	o oo	x o o	xo o o	xxo	xxo
123	2 1	231	213 4	2 3	132	231

Verse 1

     A   E7   A   E7
There's a song in the air! There's a star in the sky!

     A   E   B7   E
There's a mother's deep prayer and a baby's low cry!

     A   E7
And the star rains its fire while the beautiful sing,

     A7   D   Dm E7   A
For the manger of Bethle-hem cradles a King!

Verse 2

     A   E7   A   E7
There's a tumult of joy o'er the wonderful birth,

     A   E   B7   E
For the virgin's sweet boy is the Lord of the earth.

     A   E7
Ay! The star rains its fire while the beautiful sing,

     A7   D   Dm E7   A
For the manger of Bethle-hem cradles a King!

Verse 3

```
         A          E7         A         E7
In the light of that star lie the ages im-pearled;

          A          E          B7       E
And that song from a-far has swept over the world.

          A                    E7
Ev'ry hearth is aflame, and the beautiful sing

         A7         D      Dm E7      A
In the homes of the nations that Jesus is King!
```

Verse 4

```
         A          E7         A         E7
We re-joice in the light, and we echo the song

            A           E          B7       E
That comes down through the night from the heavenly throng.

          A              E7
Ay! We shout to the lovely e-vangel they bring,

         A7          D      Dm E7        A
And we greet in His cradle our Savior and King!
```

To Us Is Born a Little Child

Traditional German Carol

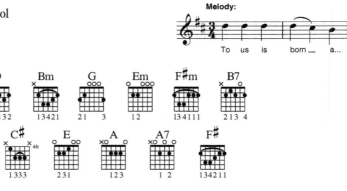

Verse 1

```
D    Bm  G D G D
To us is born a lit - tle Child
```

```
Bm G  Em D    F#m  B7 C#
Of_ Ma-ry, maiden Moth - er mild,
```

```
E    A   D G  A D   A7 F#
Yule-time a mer-ry sea - son is,
```

```
A    D    A      G  A7 D
Babe Jesus our de - light and bliss.
```

Chorus 1

```
D  A7 G   A7 D D7 G
O Je - sus dar - ling of my heart,
```

```
D    A    G   A7  D
How rich in mercy, Babe, Thou art.
```

Verse 2

```
D                Bm  G D   G D
```
Strange sight with-in__ a sta - ble old,

```
Bm  G  Em D    F#m B7 C#
```
Lo,_ God is_born in want and cold,

```
E  A   D  G    A   D   A7 F#
```
O self - ish world this Babe, I_ say,

```
A   D      A   G   A7 D
```
Doth put thee to the blush to - day.

Chorus 2   Repeat Chorus 1

Verse 3

```
D          Bm  G D    G  D
```
Now angels' joy - ful hymns up-raise,

```
Bm  G   Em  D     F#m  B7 C#
```
And God's own Son with car - ols praise.

```
E  A   D G   A D   A7   F#
```
To Beth-le-hem the shep-herds fare,

```
A   D      A    G    A7 D
```
And firstlings of their flock they bear.

Chorus 3   Repeat Chorus 1

'Twas the Night Before Christmas

Words by Clement Clark Moore
Music by F. Henri Klickman

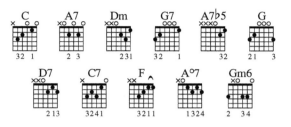

Verse 1

          C   A7   Dm   G7
'Twas the night before Christmas, when all through the house,

    Dm   G7   C
Not a creature was stirring, not even a mouse.

                       A7♭5   G
The stockings were hung by the chimney with care,

        D7   G7
In the hopes that Saint Nicholas soon would be there.

         C   A7   Dm   G7
The children were nestled all snug in their beds,

    Dm   G7   C   C7
While visions of sugar plums danced through their heads.

      F   A°7   C Gm6 A7
And mamma in her 'kerchief, and I__ in my cap,

        D7   G7   C
Had just settled our brains for a long winter's nap.

Verse 2

       C   A7   Dm   G7
When out on the lawn there a-rose such a clatter,

Dm   G7   C
I sprang from the bed to see what was the matter.

              A7♭5   G
Away to the window I flew like a flash,

     D7   G7
Tore open the shutters and threw up the sash.

      C   A7   Dm   G7
The moon on the breast of the new-fallen snow

     Dm   G7   C   C7
Gave a lustre of midday to objects be-low.

     F   A°7   C Gm6   A7
When, what to my wondering eyes should ap - pear,

    D7   G7   C
But a miniature sleigh and eight tiny rein - deer,

Verse 3

       C   A7   Dm   G7
With a little old driver, so lively and quick,

Dm   G7   C
I knew in a moment it must be St. Nick.

             A7♭5   G
More rapid than eagles his coursers they came,

    D7   G7
And he whistled, and shouted, and called them by name:

      C   A7   Dm   G7
"Now, Dasher! Now, Dancer! Now, Prancer and Vixen!

    Dm   G7   C   C7
On, Comet! On Cupid! On, Donner and Blitzen!

     F   A°7   C Gm6 A7
To the top of the porch, to the top of the wall!

    D7   G7   C
Now dash away! Dash away! Dash away all!"

Verse 4

       C   A7   Dm   G7
As dry leaves that be-fore the wild hurricane fly,

          Dm   G7   C
When they meet with an obstacle, mount to the sky,

                   A7♭5   G
So up to the house top the coursers they flew,

         D7   G7
With the sleigh full of toys, and St. Nicholas too.

       C   A7   Dm   G7
And then, in a twinkling, I heard on the roof

    Dm   G7   C   C7
The prancing and pawing of each little hoof.

    F   A°7   C Gm6 A7
As I drew in my hand, and was turn - ing a - round,

       D7   G7   C
Down the chimney St. Nicholas came with a bound.

Verse 5

       C   A7   Dm   G7
He was dressed all in fur, from his head to his foot,

          Dm   G7   C
And his clothes were all tarnished with ashes and soot;

                   A7♭5   G
A bundle of toys he had flung on his back,

        D7   G7
And he looked like a peddler just opening his pack.

       C   A7   Dm   G7
His eyes, how they twinkled! His dimples, how merry!

   Dm   G7   C   C7
His cheeks were like roses, his nose like a cherry!

    F   A°7   C Gm6 A7
His droll little mouth was drawn up like a bow,

       D7   G7   C
And the beard of his chin was as white as the snow.

Verse 6

     C   A7   Dm   G7
The stump of a pipe he held tight in his teeth,

     Dm   G7   C
And the smoke, it en - circled his head like a wreath.

                 A7♭5   G
He had a broad face and a little round belly

     D7   G7
That shook, when he laughed, like a bowl full of jelly.

     C   A7   Dm   G7
He was chubby and plump, a right jolly old elf,

     Dm   G7   C   C7
And I laughed when I saw him, in spite of my-self;

  F   A°7   C   Gm6 A7
A wink of his eye, and a twist of his head,

     D7   G7   C
Soon gave me to know I had nothing to dread.

Verse 7

     C   A7   Dm   G7
He spoke not a word, but went straight to his work,

     Dm   G7   C
And filled all the stockings; then turned with a jerk,

              A7♭5   G
And laying his finger a - side of his nose,

     D7   G7
And giving a nod, up the chimney he rose.

     C   A7   Dm   G7
He sprang to his sleigh, to his team gave a whistle,

     Dm   G7   C   C7
And a-way they all fled like the down of a thistle.

     F   A°7   C   Gm6 A7
But I heard him ex - claim, ere he drove out of sight,

     D7   G7   C
"Happy Christmas to all, and to all a good night!"

The Twelve Days of Christmas

Traditional English Carol

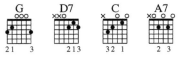

Verse 1

         G   **D7**   **G**
On the first day of Christmas, my true love sent to me

        D7   **G C G**
A partridge in a pear tree._____

Verse 2

         G   **D7**   **G**
On the second day of Christmas, my true love sent to me

D7
Two turtle doves

    G   **D7**   **G C G**
And a partridge in a pear tree.____

Verse 3

         G   **D7**   **G**
On the third day of Christmas, my true love sent to me

D7
Three French hens...

Etc., counting back to "A partridge in a pear tree"

Verse 4

         G   **D7**   **G**
On the fourth day of Christmas, my true love sent to me

D7
Four calling birds...

| | G | D7 | G |

Verse 5

On the fifth day of Christmas, my true love sent to me

A7 **D7**

Five golden rings...

G   **D7**   **G**

Verse 6

On the sixth day of Christmas, my true love gave to me

D7

Six geese a-laying...

G   **D7**   **G**

Verse 7

On the seventh day of Christmas, my true love gave to me

D7

Seven swans a-swimming...

G   **D7**   **G**

Verse 8

On the eighth day of Christmas, my true love gave to me

D7

Eight maids a-milking...

G   **D7**   **G**

Verse 9

On the ninth day of Christmas, my true love gave to me

D7

Nine ladies dancing...

G   **D7**   **G**

Verse 10

On the tenth day of Christmas, my true love gave to me

D7

Ten lords a-leaping...

G   **D7**   **G**

Verse 11

On the eleventh day of Christmas, my true love gave to me

D7

Eleven pipers piping...

G   **D7**   **G**

Verse 12

On the twelfth day of Christmas, my true love gave to me

D7

Twelve drummers drumming...

Up on the Housetop

Words and Music by
B.R. Handy

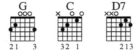

Verse 1

G
Up on the housetop reindeer pause,

C   G   D7
Out jumps good old Santa Claus;

G
Down through the chimney with lots of toys,

C   G   D7   G
All for the little ones, Christmas joys.

Chorus 1

C   G
Ho, ho, ho! Who wouldn't go?

D7   G
Ho, ho, ho! Who wouldn't go?

C   G   C
Up on the housetop, click, click, click,

G   D7   G
Down through the chimney with good Saint Nick.

Verse 2   **G**
First comes the stocking of little Nell;

C   **G**   **D7**
Oh, dear Santa, fill it well.

G
Give her a dolly that laughs and cries,

C   **G**   **D7**   **G**
One that will open and shut her eyes.

Chorus 2   Repeat Chorus 1

Verse 3   **G**
Look in the stocking of little Will,

C   **G**   **D7**
Oh, just see what a glorious fill!

G
Here is a hammer and lots of tacks,

C   **G**   **D7**   **G**
Whistle and ball and a whip that cracks.

Chorus 3   Repeat Chorus 1

Wassail Song

Traditional English Carol

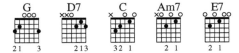

Verse 1

    G   D7   G   D7
Here we come a-wassail-ing

      G   D7   G
A - mong the leaves so green.

  C   G   D7
Here we come a wand'ring,

    Am7   D7
So fair to be seen.

Chorus 1

        G C   G
Love and joy come to you,

  D7   G   C   G
And to you glad Christmas too.

  D7   G   E7   Am7 D7 G   C
And God bless you and send you a happy New Year,

         G   E7   Am7   D7   G
And God send you a hap - py New Year.

GUITAR CHORD SONGBOOK

Verse 2

G   D7   G   D7
We are not dai - ly beg - gars

G   D7   G
That beg from door to door

C   G   D7
But we are neighbor children

Am7   D7
Whom you have seen be-fore.

Chorus 2   Repeat Chorus 1

Verse 3

G   D7 G   D7
We have got a little purse

G   D7   G
Of stretching leather skin.

C   G   D7
We want a little money

Am7   D7
To line it well with - in:

Chorus 3   Repeat Chorus 1

Verse 4

G   D7   G   D7
God bless the master of this house,

G   D7   G
Like-wise the mistress too;

C   G   D7
And all the little children

Am7   D7
That 'round the table go:

Chorus 4   Repeat Chorus 1

Watchman, Tell Us of the Night

Traditional

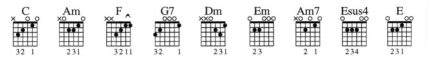

Verse 1

    C   Am C F G7   C
Watchman, tell us of the night,

       Dm C G7   C
What its signs of promise are.

    Am C   F   G7   C
Trav'ler, o'er yon mountain's height,

      Dm C G7   C
See that glo - ry beaming star.

G7   C   Em Am7 D7   G
Watchman, does its beau - teous ray

Dm   Am Esus4 E   Am
Aught of joy or hope fore-tell?

C   F   G Am7 D7 G
Trav'ler, yes, it brings the day,

F   C   DmC G7   C
Prom-ised day of Isra - el.

Verse 2

```
       C    Am  C   F G7   C
```
Watchman, tell us of the night,

```
           Dm C   G7    C
```
Higher yet that star as-cends.

```
           Am  C     F G7     C
```
Trav'ler, bless-ed-ness and light,

```
              Dm   C G7        C
```
Peace and truth, its course por-tends.

```
       G7          C Em Am7  D7 G
```
Watchman, will its beams a - lone

```
       Dm     Am    Esus4 E   Am
```
Gild the spot that gave them birth!

```
       C       F  G Am7 D7 G
```
Trav'ler, a - ges are_ its_ own;

```
       F   C Dm   C   G7    C
```
See it bursts o'er all the earth.

Verse 3

```
       C    Am  C   F G7   C
```
Watchman, tell us of the night,

```
           Dm   C  G7    C
```
For the morn-ing seems to dawn.

```
           Am C    F    G7     C
```
Trav'ler, dark-ness takes its flight,

```
           Dm C  G7      C
```
Doubt and ter-ror are with-drawn.

```
       G7          C Em Am7  D7  G
```
Watchman, let thy wand'rings cease,

```
       Dm     Am    Esus4 E Am
```
Hie thee to thy qui - et home.

```
       C       F  G Am7 D7 G
```
Trav'ler, lo, the Prince of Peace,

```
       F   C Dm   C G7    C
```
Lo, the Son of God is come.

We Are Singing

Traditional Venezuelan Folk Carol

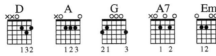

Chorus 1

   D   **A**
Singing, we are singing

D   **A** **D**
Loving praise we bring,

          G
Merry eve of Christmas,

A7   **D**
Merry eve of Christmas,

      A7 D G
Merry eve of Christmas,

A7   **D**
To Thee, Infant King.

Verse 1

   D   **Em G**
All our expec - ta - tion,

Em   **A7**   **D**
All our chari-ty,

           Em
All our conso - lation,

A7   **D**
Child dear in Thee.

GUITAR CHORD SONGBOOK

Chorus 2   Repeat Chorus 1

Verse 2
      D   **Em** **G**
Beaming through the dark-ness,

Em   **A7**   **D**
Flooding rays so bright,

               Em
Shining on the cradle,

A7   **D**
On the glorious night.

Chorus 3   Repeat Chorus 1

Verse 3
      D   **Em** **G**
Night of cele - bra - tion,

Em   **A7**   **D**
Night of Jesus' birth,

               Em
Night of holy splendor,

A7   **D**
And redeeming love.

Chorus 4   Repeat Chorus 1

We Three Kings of Orient Are

Words and Music by
John H. Hopkins, Jr.

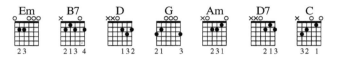

Verse 1

   Em   B7 Em
   We three kings of Orient are;

        B7   Em
   Bearing gifts we traverse a-far,

      D   G
   Field and fountain, moor and mountain,

   Am B7 Em
   Following yonder star.

Chorus 1

   D7 G   C   G
   O___ star of wonder, star of night,

        C   G
   Star with royal beauty bright,

   Em   D   C   D
   Westward leading, still pro-ceeding,

   G   C   G
   Guide us to thy perfect light.

Verse 2

   Em   B7   Em
   Born a King on Bethlehem's plain,

        B7   Em
   Gold I bring to crown Him a-gain,

      D G
   King for-ever, ceasing never

   Am B7 Em
   Over us all to reign.

Chorus 2   Repeat Chorus 1

Verse 3
```
            Em              B7      Em
```
Frankincense to offer have I;

```
                    B7      Em
```
Incense owns a Deity nigh;

```
                    D       G
```
Prayer and praising, all men raising,

```
            Am          B7      Em
```
Worship Him, God most high.

Chorus 3   Repeat Chorus 1

Verse 4
```
            Em              B7      Em
```
Myrrh is mine; its bitter per-fume

```
                    B7          Em
```
Breathes a life of gathering gloom;

```
                    D       G
```
Sorr'wing, sighing, bleeding, dying,

```
            Am          B7          Em
```
Sealed in the stone-cold tomb.

Chorus 4   Repeat Chorus 1

Verse 5
```
            Em              B7          Em
```
Glorious now, be-hold Him a-rise,

```
                    B7      Em
```
King and God and sacri-fice,

```
                    D   G
```
Alle-luia, alleluia,

```
            Am          B7      Em
```
Earth to hea-v'n re-plies.

Chorus 5   Repeat Chorus 1

We Wish You a Merry Christmas

Traditional English Folksong

G   C   A7   D   B7   Em   D7

Chorus 1
     G   **C**
We wish you a merry Christmas,

     A7   **D**
We wish you a merry Christmas,

     B7   **Em**
We wish you a merry Christmas,

     C   **D7** **G**
And a happy New Year.

Verse 1

```
           G         D       A7          D
Good tidings we bring to you and your kin.

G    D7      G              C    D7  G
Good tidings for Christmas and a happy New Year.
```

Chorus 2

```
           G                 C
We all know that Santa's coming,

           A7                D
We all know that Santa's coming,

           B7                Em
We all know that Santa's coming,

           C        D7 G
And soon will be here.
```

Verse 2   Repeat Verse 1

Chorus 3   Repeat Chorus 1

Welsh Carol

Words by Pastor K.E. Roberts
Traditional Welsh Carol

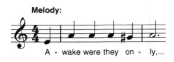

Melody:

A - wake were they on - ly,...

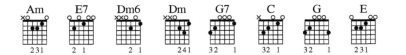

Am   E7   Dm6   Dm   G7   C   G   E

Verse 1

    Am   **E7 Am**
A-wake were they on - ly,

E7   Am   **Dm6 Dm**
Those shepherds so lone - ly,

E7 Am   **E7 Am E7   Am**
On guard in that si - lence pro - found,

E7   Am   **E7   Am**
When color had fad - ed,

E7   Am   **Dm6 Dm**
When nighttime had shad - ed

E7   Am   **E7 Am E7 Am**
Their senses from sight and from sound.

Chorus 1

```
G7 C                  G
```
Lo, then broke a won - der,

```
Am   E   Am      E
```
Then drift-ed asun-der

```
     Am        E Am   Dm6  Am   E
```
The veils from the splen - dor__ of__ God,

```
        Am        E7 Am
```
When light from the Ho - ly,

```
E7   Am          Dm6 Dm
```
Came down to the low - ly,

```
E7  Am          E7   Am E7 Am
```
And heav'n to the earth that they trod.

```
G7  C               G
```
O,_ spirit all-know - ing,

```
Am   E      Am        E
```
Thou source overflow - ing,

```
   Am      E  Am Dm6 Am E
```
O move in the dark-ness_ a - round,

```
        Am        E7 Am
```
That sight may be in_ us,

```
E7   Am          Dm6 Dm
```
True hearing to win_ us,

```
E7   Am           E7    Am E7 Am
```
Glad tidings where Christ may be found.

Verse 2

```
      Am        E7 Am
```
May light now en-fold us,

```
E7   Am          Dm6  Dm
```
O_ Lord, for be - hold_ us,

```
E7   Am               E7  Am E7   Am
```
Like shepherds from tu - mult with - drawn,

```
E7   Am          E7   Am
```
Nor heaving, nor see - ing,

```
E7  Am        Dm6 Dm
```
All other care flee - ing,

```
E7   Am          E7  Am E7 Am
```
We wait the in - eff - a - ble dawn.

Chorus 2   Repeat Chorus 1

What Child Is This?

Words by William C. Dix
16th Century English Melody

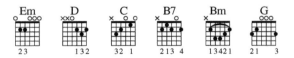

Em   D   C   B7   Bm   G

Em D		

Verse 1

         Em   **D**
What Child is this, who, laid to rest,

         C   **B7**
On Mary's lap is sleeping?

         Em   **D**
Whom angels greet with anthems sweet,

         C   **B7**   **Em**
While shepherds watch are keeping?

Chorus 1

         Bm G   **D**   **Bm**
This, this is Christ the King,

         Em   **C**   **B7**
Whom shepherds guard and angels sing:

         G   **D**   **Bm**
Haste, haste to bring Him laud,

         Em   **B7**   **Em**
The Babe, the Son of Mary.

Verse 2

      Em   D
Why lies He in such mean estate

      C   B7
Where ox and ass are feeding?

      Em   D
Good Christian, fear, for sinners here

      C   B7   Em
The silent Word is pleading.

Chorus 2   Repeat Chorus 1

Verse 3

      Em   D
So bring Him incense, gold, and myrrh,

      C   B7
Come peasant king to own Him;

      Em   D
The King of kings sal-vation brings,

      C   B7   Em
Let loving hearts en-throne Him.

Chorus 3   Repeat Chorus 1

When Christ Was Born of Mary Free

Traditional English Carol

Melody:

When Christ was born of ___ Mar - y ___ free,...

G   D   Bm   Em   Am   D7   A7   Dm   C   Am7

Verse 1

G   D   Bm Em   Am D7 G
When Christ was born of Mar - y free,

D7   G   Em A7 D
In Bethle-hem that fair cit - y,

Dm   Am   C   G
An - gels sung there with mirth and glee:

D7   G
"In excelsis glori - a."

Chorus 1

G   C   G
In excelsis glori - a,

D   Am7 D7 G   D7 G
In ex - cel - sis glo - ri - a,

Em C G   Am D
In ex - cel - sis glo - ri - a.

G   Em G   D7 G
In excel-sis glo - ri - a.

Verse 2

G   D   Bm Em   Am D7 G
This King is_ come to save man-kind,

　　　D7   G　　　Em   A7 D
As in the scripture truths we find,

　　　Dm   Am   C   G
There-fore this song we have in mind:

　　　　　D7   G
"In excelsis glori - a."

Chorus 2   Repeat Chorus 1

Verse 3

G   D   Bm Em   Am D7   G
Then, dear-est Lord, for Thy great grace,

　　　D7   G　　Em A7   D
Grant us in bliss to see Thy face,

　　　Dm   Am   C   G
That we may sing to Thy so-lace:

　　　　　D7   G
"In excelsis glori - a."

Chorus 3   Repeat Chorus 1

Whence Comes This Rush of Wings

Traditional French Carol

Whence comes this rush of wings a-far,...

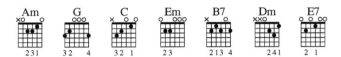

Verse 1

    Am   G   C   G
Whence comes this rush of wings a-far,

    Am   G   Am Em B7 Em
Following straight the No - ël_ star?

    Am   G   C   G
Birds from the woods in wondrous flight,

    C   Dm Am E7 Am
Bethlehem seek this ho - ly night.

Verse 2

    Am   G   C   G
"Tell us, ye birds, why come ye here,

    Am   G Am Em B7 Em
Into this sta-ble_ poor and drear?"

    Am   G   C   G
"Hast'ning we seek the Newborn King,

    C   Dm Am E7 Am
And all our sweet-est mu - sic bring."

Verse 3

Am   G   C   G
Hark how the green finch bears his part,

Am   G   Am Em B7 Em
Philomel, too, with ten - der heart

Am   G C   G
Chants from her leafy dark re-treat,

C   Dm Am E7   Am
"Re mi fa sol" in___ ac - cents sweet.

Verse 4

Am   G   C   G
Angels and shepherds, birds of the sky,

Am   G Am Em B7 Em
Come where the Son of___ God doth lie.

Am   G   C   G
Christ on earth with man doth dwell,

C   Dm Am E7 Am
Join in the shout, "No - ël, No - ël."

While by My Sheep

Traditional German Carol

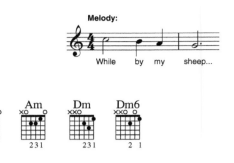

Melody:

While by my sheep...

C   G   F   E7   Am   Dm   Dm6

Verse 1

    C G F C   F   G C
While by my sheep I watched at night,

    G F   C   F G C
Glad tid-ings brought an an-gel bright.

Chorus 1

    E7   Am E7   Am
How great my joy, great my joy.

    G   C Am G C
Joy, joy, joy, joy, joy, joy!

    Dm   E7   F Dm6 E7 Am
Praise to the Lord in heav'n on high.

Verse 2
```
   C   G   F C      F G C
There shall be born, so he did say,

   G   F C   F   G   C
In Beth-le-hem, a Child to - day.
```

Chorus 2   Repeat Chorus 1

Verse 3
```
   C   G   F C   F   G   C
There shall He lie, in man-ger mean,

   G   F C      F   G   C
Who shall re-deem the world from sin.
```

Chorus 3   Repeat Chorus 1

Verse 4
```
   C   G F C      F G C
Lord, ev-er-more to me be nigh,

   G   F C      F   G   C
Then shall my heart be filled with joy!
```

Chorus 4   Repeat Chorus 1

CHRISTMAS CAROLS

While Shepherds Watched Their Flocks

Words by Nahum Tate
Music by George Frideric Handel

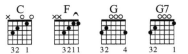

Verse 1

    C   F   C
While shepherds watched their flocks by night,

             G
All seated on the ground,

   G7   C
The angel of the Lord came down,

    F   G7   C
And glory shone a-round.

Verse 2

    C   F   C
"Fear not," said he, for mighty dread

              G
Had seized their troubled mind.

   G7   C
"Glad tidings of great joy I bring

    F   G7   C
To you and all man-kind.

GUITAR CHORD SONGBOOK

Verse 3

    C   F   C
"To you in David's town this day

                G
Is born of David's line

  G7   C
A Savior, who is Christ the Lord,

    F   G7   C
And this shall be the sign.

Verse 4

    C   F   C
"The heav'nly babe you there shall find

               G
To human view dis-played,

  G7   C
All meanly wrapped in swathing bands

    F G7   C
And in a manger laid."

Verse 5

    C   F   C
Thus spoke the seraph, and forthwith

               G
Appeared a shining throng

  G7   C
Of angels praising God on high,

    F   G7   C
Who thus ad-dressed their song:

Verse 6

    C   F   C
"All glory be to God on high,

               G
And on the earth be peace;

  G7   C
Good-will henceforth from heav'n to earth

    F   G7 C
Be-gin and never cease!"

Yuletide Is Here Again

Traditional Swedish Dance Carol

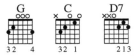

Verse 1

    G
Yuletide is here again,

The yuletide is here again,

Let's celebrate, rejoice till Easter.

C
Then when it's Eastertime,

    G
Yes, then, when it's Eastertime,

      D7   **G**
We'll celebrate, rejoice till Christ-mas.

Verse 2

G
Yuletide is here again,

The yuletide is here again,

Let's celebrate, rejoice till Easter.

C   **G**
Ev'ryone knows this really cannot be so,

           D7   **G**
Because of Lent, when we all must start fast-ing.

Wexford Carol

Traditional Irish Carol

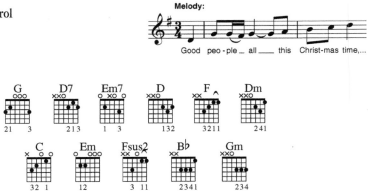

Verse 1

        G   **D7**   **G**
Good people all,__ this Christmas time,

     D7 Em7 D   **F**   **Dm** **D**
Con-sider well__ and bear in mind,__

       G   **D7**   **G**
What our good God__ for us has done

   C   **Em D**   **C**   **G**
In sending His____ be-loved Son.

     Fsus2 F **B♭**
With Mary holy we should pray

    Gm   **C**   **Dm**   **D**
To God with love__ this Christmas day;__

    G   **D7**   **G**
In Bethlehem__ up-on that morn

      C   **Em** **D**   **C G**
There was a blessed__ Mes-siah born.

GUITAR CHORD SONGBOOK

Verse 2

  G   **D7** **G**
The night before__ that happy tide

  D7 **Em7 D** **F** **Dm D**
The noble Vir - gin and her guide__

   G   **D7** **G**
Were long time seek - ing up and down

  C **Em D** **C** **G**
To find a lodg - ing in the town.

  Fsus2 **F**   **B♭**
But mark how all things came to pass:

  Gm   **C**   **Dm**   **D**
From ev'ry door__ re - pelled, alas!__

 G   **D7** **G**
As long foretold,__ their refuge all

   C **Em D** **C** **G**
Was but a hum - ble ox's stall.

Verse 3

   G   **D7** **G**
Near Bethlehem__ did shepherds keep

  D7 **Em7 D** **F**   **Dm D**
Their flocks of lambs__ and feeding sheep;__

  G   **D7** **G**
To whom God's an - gels did appear,

   C **Em D** **C** **G**
Which put the shep - herds in great fear.

  Fsus2 **F**   **B♭**
"Pre-pare and go," the angels said,

  Gm   **C** **Dm**   **D**
"To Bethlehem,__ be not afraid;___

  G   **D7** **G**
For there you'll find,__ this happy morn,

  C   **Em D**   **C** **G**
A princely babe,__ sweet Jesus born."

Verse 4

```
        G           D7      G
With thankful heart__ and joyful mind,
        D7      Em7 D    F      Dm  D
The shepherds went__ the Babe to find,___
        G           D7  G
And as God's an - gel had foretold,
        C       Em D   C       G
They did our Sav - ior Christ be-hold.
        Fsus2 F      B♭
With-in a__ manger He was laid,
        Gm      C     Dm        D
And by His side__ the Virgin maid,___
        G       D7      G
At-tending on__ the Lord of life,
        C       Em D   C       G
Who came on earth__ to end all strife.
```

Verse 5

```
        G           D7        G
There were three wise___ men from afar
        D7   Em7 D F       Dm  D
Di-rected by___ a glorious star,___
        G           D7      G
And on they wan - dered night and day
        C       Em D     C    G
Un-til they came__ where Jesus lay,
        Fsus2      F      B♭
And when they came un-to that place
        Gm      C     Dm      D
Where our beloved__ Mes-siah was,___
        G       D7      G
They humbly cast__ them at His feet,
        C       Em D   C       G
With gifts of gold___ and incense sweet.
```

Guitar Chord Songbooks

Each book includes complete lyrics, chord symbols, and guitar chord diagrams.

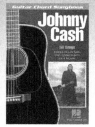  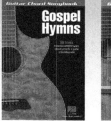 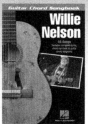

Acoustic Hits
More than 60 songs: Against the Wind • Name • One • Southern Cross • Take Me Home, Country Roads • Teardrops on My Guitar • Who'll Stop the Rain • Ziggy Stardust • and more.
00701787 ....$14.99

Acoustic Rock
80 acoustic favorites: Blackbird • Blowin' in the Wind • Layla • Maggie May • Me and Julio down by the Schoolyard • Pink Houses • and more.
00699540..................................$21.99

Alabama
50 of Alabama's best: Angels Among Us • The Closer You Get • If You're Gonna Play in Texas (You Gotta Have a Fiddle in the Band) • Mountain Music • When We Make Love • and more.
00699914..................................$14.95

The Beach Boys
59 favorites: California Girls • Don't Worry Baby • Fun, Fun, Fun • Good Vibrations • Help Me Rhonda • Wouldn't It Be Nice • dozens more!
00699566..................................$19.99

The Beatles
100 more Beatles hits: Lady Madonna • Let It Be • Ob-La-Di, Ob-La-Da • Paperback Writer • Revolution • Twist and Shout • When I'm Sixty-Four • and more.
00699562..................................$17.99

Bluegrass
Over 40 classics: Blue Moon of Kentucky • Foggy Mountain Top • High on a Mountain Top • Keep on the Sunny Side • Wabash Cannonball • The Wreck of the Old '97 • and more.
00702585..................................$14.99

Johnny Cash
58 Cash classics: A Boy Named Sue • Cry, Cry, Cry • Daddy Sang Bass • Folsom Prison Blues • I Walk the Line • Ring of Fire • Solitary Man • and more.
00699648..................................$17.99

Children's Songs
70 songs for kids: Alphabet Song • Bingo • The Candy Man • Eensy Weensy Spider • Puff the Magic Dragon • Twinkle, Twinkle Little Star • and more.
00699539..................................$16.99

Christmas Carols
80 Christmas carols: Angels We Have Heard on High • The Holly and the Ivy • I Saw Three Ships • Joy to the World • O Holy Night • and more.
00699536..................................$12.99

Christmas Songs
80 songs: All I Want for Christmas Is My Two Front Teeth • Baby, It's Cold Outside • Jingle Bell Rock • Mistletoe and Holly • Sleigh Ride • and more.
00119911..................................$14.99

Eric Clapton
75 of Slowhand's finest: I Shot the Sheriff • Knockin' on Heaven's Door • Layla • Strange Brew • Tears in Heaven • Wonderful Tonight • and more.
00699567 ....$19.99

Classic Rock
80 rock essentials: Beast of Burden • Cat Scratch Fever • Hot Blooded • Money • Rhiannon • Sweet Emotion • Walk on the Wild Side • and more.
00699598 ....$18.99

Coffeehouse Hits
57 singer-songwriter hits: Don't Know Why • Hallelujah • Meet Virginia • Steal My Kisses • Torn • Wonderwall • You Learn • and more.
00703318 ....$14.99

Country
80 country standards: Boot Scootin' Boogie • Crazy • Hey, Good Lookin'• Sixteen Tons • Through the Years • Your Cheatin' Heart • and more.
00699534 ....$17.99

Country Favorites
Over 60 songs: Achy Breaky Heart (Don't Tell My Heart) • Brand New Man • Gone Country • The Long Black Veil • Make the World Go Away • and more.
00700609 ....$14.99

Country Hits
40 classics: As Good As I Once Was • Before He Cheats • Cruise • Follow Your Arrow • God Gave Me You • The House That Built Me • Just a Kiss • Making Memories of Us • Need You Now • Your Man • and more.
00140859 ....$14.99

Country Standards
60 songs: By the Time I Get to Phoenix • El Paso • The Gambler • I Fall to Pieces • Jolene • King of the Road • Put Your Hand in the Hand • A Rainy Night in Georgia • and more.
00700608 ....$12.95

Cowboy Songs
Over 60 tunes: Back in the Saddle Again • Happy Trails • Home on the Range • Streets of Laredo • The Yellow Rose of Texas • and more.
00699636 ....$19.99

Creedence Clearwater Revival
34 CCR classics: Bad Moon Rising • Born on the Bayou • Down on the Corner • Fortunate Son • Up Around the Bend • and more.
00701786 ....$16.99

Jim Croce
37 tunes: Bad, Bad Leroy Brown • I Got a Name • I'll Have to Say I Love You in a Song • Operator (That's Not the Way It Feels) • Photographs and Memories • Time in a Bottle • You Don't Mess Around with Jim • and many more.
00148087 ....$14.99

Complete contents listings available online at www.halleonard.com

Crosby, Stills & Nash
37 hits: Chicago • Dark Star • Deja Vu • Marrakesh Express • Our House • Southern Cross • Suite: Judy Blue Eyes • Teach Your Children • and more.
00701609................................$16.99

John Denver
50 favorites: Annie's Song • Leaving on a Jet Plane • Rocky Mountain High • Take Me Home, Country Roads • Thank God I'm a Country Boy • and more.
02501697................................$17.99

Neil Diamond
50 songs: America • Cherry, Cherry • Cracklin' Rosie • Forever in Blue Jeans • I Am...I Said • Love on the Rocks • Song Sung Blue • Sweet Caroline • and dozens more!
00700606 ....$19.99

Disney
56 super Disney songs: Be Our Guest • Friend like Me • Hakuna Matata • It's a Small World • Under the Sea • A Whole New World • Zip-A-Dee-Doo-Dah • and more.
00701071 ....$17.99

The Doors
60 classics from the Doors: Break on Through to the Other Side • Hello, I Love You (Won't You Tell Me Your Name?) • Light My Fire • Love Her Madly • Riders on the Storm • Touch Me • and more.
00699888 ....$17.99

Eagles
40 familiar songs: Already Gone • Best of My Love • Desperado • Hotel California • Life in the Fast Lane • Peaceful Easy Feeling • Witchy Woman • more.
00122917 ....$16.99

Early Rock
80 classics: All I Have to Do Is Dream • Big Girls Don't Cry • Fever • Itsy Bitsy Teenie Weenie Yellow Polkadot Bikini • Let's Twist Again • Lollipop • and more.
00699916 ....$14.99

Folk Pop Rock
80 songs: American Pie • Dust in the Wind • Me and Bobby McGee • Somebody to Love • Time in a Bottle • and more.
00699651 ....$17.99

Folksongs
80 folk favorites: Aura Lee • Camptown Races • Danny Boy • Man of Constant Sorrow • Nobody Knows the Trouble I've Seen • and more.
00699541 ....$14.99

40 Easy Strumming Songs
Features 40 songs: Cat's in the Cradle • Daughter • Hey, Soul Sister • Homeward Bound • Take It Easy • Wild Horses • and more.
00115972 ....$16.99

Four Chord Songs
40 hit songs: Blowin' in the Wind • I Saw Her Standing There • Should I Stay or Should I Go • Stand by Me • Turn the Page • Wonderful Tonight • and more.
00701611................................$14.99

Glee
50+ hits: Bad Romance • Beautiful • Dancing with Myself • Don't Stop Believin' • Imagine • Rehab • Teenage Dream • True Colors • and dozens more.
00702501................................$14.99

Gospel Hymns
80 hymns: Amazing Grace • Give Me That Old Time Religion • I Love to Tell the Story • Shall We Gather at the River? • Wondrous Love • and more.
00700463 ....$14.99

Grand Ole Opry®
80 great songs: Abilene • Act Naturally • Country Boy • Crazy • Friends in Low Places • He Stopped Loving Her Today • Wings of a Dove • dozens more!
00699885 ....$16.95

Grateful Dead
30 favorites: Casey Jones • Friend of the Devil • High Time • Ramble on Rose • Ripple • Rosemary • Sugar Magnolia • Truckin' • Uncle John's Band • more.
00139461 ....$14.99

Green Day
34 faves: American Idiot • Basket Case • Boulevard of Broken Dreams • Good Riddance (Time of Your Life) • 21 Guns • Wake Me Up When September Ends • When I Come Around • and more.
00103074 ....$14.99

Irish Songs
45 Irish favorites: Danny Boy • Girl I Left Behind Me • Harrigan • I'll Tell Me Ma • The Irish Rover • My Wild Irish Rose • When Irish Eyes Are Smiling • and more!
00701044 ....$14.99

Michael Jackson
27 songs: Bad • Beat It • Billie Jean • Black or White (Rap Version) • Don't Stop 'Til You Get Enough • The Girl Is Mine • Man in the Mirror • Rock with You • Smooth Criminal • Thriller • more.
00137847 ....$14.99

Billy Joel
60 Billy Joel favorites: It's Still Rock and Roll to Me • The Longest Time • Piano Man • She's Always a Woman • Uptown Girl • We Didn't Start the Fire • You May Be Right • and more.
00699632 ....$19.99

Elton John
60 songs: Bennie and the Jets • Candle in the Wind • Crocodile Rock • Goodbye Yellow Brick Road • Sad Songs Say So Much • Tiny Dancer • Your Song • more.
00699732 ....$15.99

Ray LaMontagne
20 songs: Empty • Gossip in the Grain • Hold You in My Arms • I Still Care for You • Jolene • Trouble • You Are the Best Thing • and more.
00130337................................$12.99

Latin Songs
60 favorites: Bésame Mucho (Kiss Me Much) • The Girl from Ipanema (Garôta De Ipanema) • The Look of Love • So Nice (Summer Samba) • and more.
00700973 ....$14.99

Love Songs
65 romantic ditties: Baby, I'm-A Want You • Fields of Gold • Here, There and Everywhere • Let's Stay Together • Never My Love • The Way We Were • more!
00701043................................$14.99

Bob Marley
36 songs: Buffalo Soldier • Get up Stand Up • I Shot the Sheriff • Is This Love • No Woman No Cry • One Love • Redemption Song • and more.
00701704................................$17.99

Bruno Mars
15 hits: Count on Me • Grenade • If I Knew • Just the Way You Are • The Lazy Song • Locked Out of Heaven • Marry You • Treasure • When I Was Your Man • and more.
00125332 ....$12.99

Paul McCartney
60 from Sir Paul: Band on the Run • Jet • Let 'Em In • Maybe I'm Amazed • No More Lonely Nights • Say Say Say • Take It Away • With a Little Luck • and more!
00385035 ....$16.95

Steve Miller
33 hits: Dance Dance Dance • Jet Airliner • The Joker • Jungle Love • Rock'n Me • Serenade from the Stars • Swingtown • Take the Money and Run • and more.
00701146................................$12.99

Modern Worship
80 modern worship favorites: All Because of Jesus • Amazed • Everlasting God • Happy Day • I Am Free • Jesus Messiah • and more.
00701801 ....$16.99

Motown
60 Motown masterpieces: ABC • Baby I Need Your Lovin' • I'll Be There • Stop! In the Name of Love • You Can't Hurry Love • and more.
00699734 ....$17.99

Willie Nelson
44 favorites: Always on My Mind • Beer for My Horses • Blue Skies • Georgia on My Mind • Help Me Make It Through the Night • On the Road Again • Whiskey River • and many more.
00148273 ....$17.99

Nirvana
40 songs: About a Girl • Come as You Are • Heart Shaped Box • The Man Who Sold the World • Smells like Teen Spirit • You Know You're Right • and more.
00699762 ....$16.99

Roy Orbison
38 songs: Blue Bayou • Oh, Pretty Woman • Only the Lonely (Know the Way I Feel) • Working for the Man • You Got It • and more.
00699752 ....$17.99

Peter, Paul & Mary
43 favorites: If I Had a Hammer (The Hammer Song) • Leaving on a Jet Plane • Puff the Magic Dragon • This Land Is Your Land • and more.
00103013................................$19.99

Tom Petty
American Girl • Breakdown • Don't Do Me like That • Free Fallin' • Here Comes My Girl • Into the Great Wide Open • Mary Jane's Last Dance • Refugee • Runnin' Down a Dream • The Waiting • and more.
00699883 ....$15.99

Pink Floyd
30 songs: Another Brick in the Wall, Part 2 • Brain Damage • Breathe • Comfortably Numb • Hey You • Money • Mother • Run like Hell • Us and Them • Wish You Were Here • Young Lust • and many more.
00139116 ....$14.99

Pop/Rock
80 chart hits: Against All Odds • Come Sail Away • Every Breath You Take • Hurts So Good • Kokomo • More Than Words • Smooth • Summer of '69 • and more.
00699538 ....$16.99

Praise and Worship
80 favorites: Agnus Dei • He Is Exalted • I Could Sing of Your Love Forever • Lord, I Lift Your Name on High • More Precious Than Silver • Open the Eyes of My Heart • Shine, Jesus, Shine • and more.
00699634 ....$14.99

Elvis Presley
60 hits: All Shook Up • Blue Suede Shoes • Can't Help Falling in Love • Heartbreak Hotel • Hound Dog • Jailhouse Rock • Suspicious Minds • Viva Las Vegas • and more.
00699633 ....$17.99

Queen
40 hits: Bohemian Rhapsody • Crazy Little Thing Called Love • Fat Bottomed Girls • Killer Queen • Tie Your Mother Down • Under Pressure • You're My Best Friend • and more!
00702395 ....$14.99

Red Hot Chili Peppers
50 hits: Californication • Give It Away • Higher Ground • Love Rollercoaster • Scar Tissue • Suck My Kiss • Under the Bridge • and more.
00699710 ....$19.99

The Rolling Stones
35 hits: Angie • Beast of Burden • Fool to Cry • Happy • It's Only Rock 'N' Roll (But I Like It) • Miss You • Not Fade Away • Respectable • Rocks Off • Start Me Up • Time Is on My Side • Tumbling Dice • Waiting on a Friend • and more.
00137716 ....$17.99

Bob Seger
41 favorites: Against the Wind • Hollywood Nights • Katmandu • Like a Rock • Night Moves • Old Time Rock & Roll • You'll Accomp'ny Me • and more!
00701147 ....$12.99

Carly Simon
Nearly 40 classic hits, including: Anticipation • Haven't Got Time for the Pain • Jesse • Let the River Run • Nobody Does It Better • You're So Vain • and more.
00121011................................$14.99

Sting
50 favorites from Sting and the Police: Don't Stand So Close to Me • Every Breath You Take • Fields of Gold • King of Pain • Message in a Bottle • Roxanne • and more.
00699921 ....$17.99

Taylor Swift
40 tunes: Back to December • Bad Blood • Blank Space • Fearless • Fifteen • I Knew You Were Trouble • Look What You Made Me Do • Love Story • Mean • Shake It Off • Speak Now • Wildest Dreams • and many more.
00263755................................$16.99

Three Chord Acoustic Songs
30 acoustic songs: All Apologies • Blowin' in the Wind • Hold My Hand • Just the Way You Are • Ring of Fire • Shelter from the Storm • This Land Is Your Land • and more.
00123860 ....$14.99

Three Chord Songs
65 includes: All Right Now • La Bamba • Lay Down Sally • Mony, Mony • Rock Around the Clock • Rock This Town • Werewolves of London • You Are My Sunshine • and more.
00699720 ....$17.99

Two-Chord Songs
Nearly 60 songs: ABC • Brick House • Eleanor Rigby • Fever • Paperback Writer • Ramblin' Man Tulsa Time • When Love Comes to Town • and more.
00119236................................$16.99

U2
40 U2 songs: Beautiful Day • Mysterious Ways • New Year's Day • One • Sunday Bloody Sunday • Walk On • Where the Streets Have No Name • With or Without You • and more.
00137744................................$14.99

Hank Williams
68 classics: Cold, Cold Heart • Hey, Good Lookin' • Honky Tonk Blues • I'm a Long Gone Daddy • Jambalaya (On the Bayou) • Your Cheatin' Heart • and more.
00700607 ....$16.99

Stevie Wonder
40 of Stevie's best: For Once in My Life • Higher Ground • Isn't She Lovely • My Cherie Amour • Sir Duke • Superstition • Uptight (Everything's Alright) • Yester-Me, Yester-You, Yesterday • and more!
00120862 ....$14.99

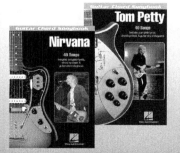

HAL•LEONARD®

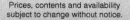

Prices, contents and availability subject to change without notice.

Complete contents listings available online at www.halleonard.com